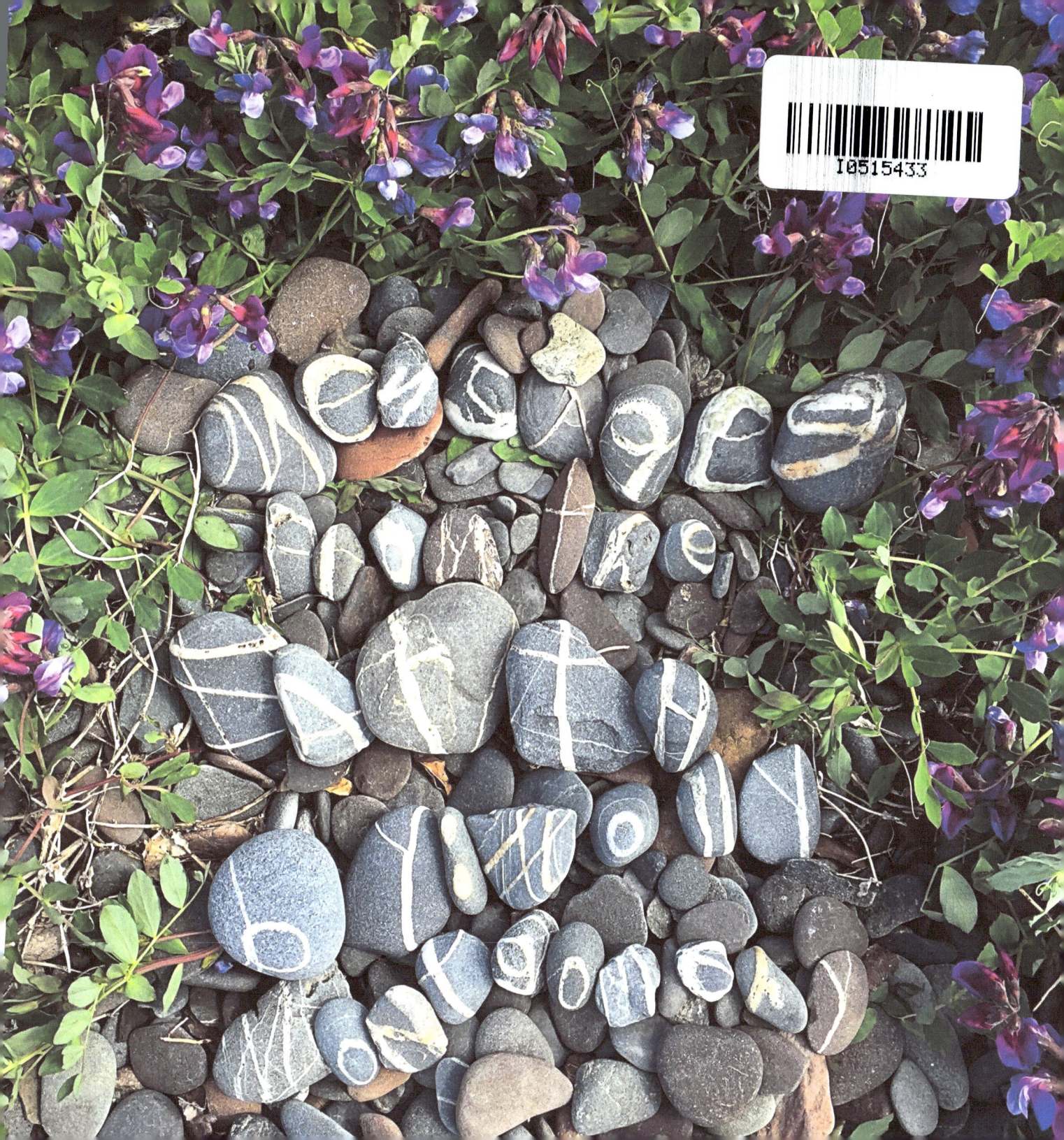

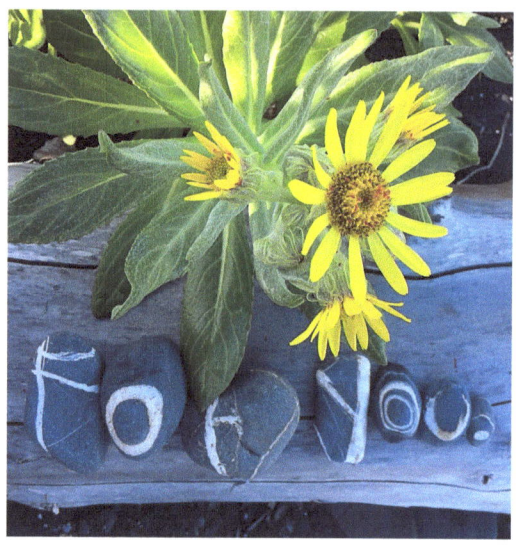

Messages from the Earth

Copyright ©2017 by Molly Montgomery. All rights reserved.
No part of this book may be used or reproduced in any manner whatsoever without written permission from the author, except in the case of brief quotations embodied in critical articles and reviews.

Book design, photographs and illustrations by Molly Montgomery

Printed in the United States of America
First print edition: September 2017

Available on amazon.com or through your local bookstore.
A Beachcomber product from Molly Montgomery;
more information at www.ibeachcomber.com

All images in this book occurred or were created naturally
(including rocks used for coloring on other rocks).

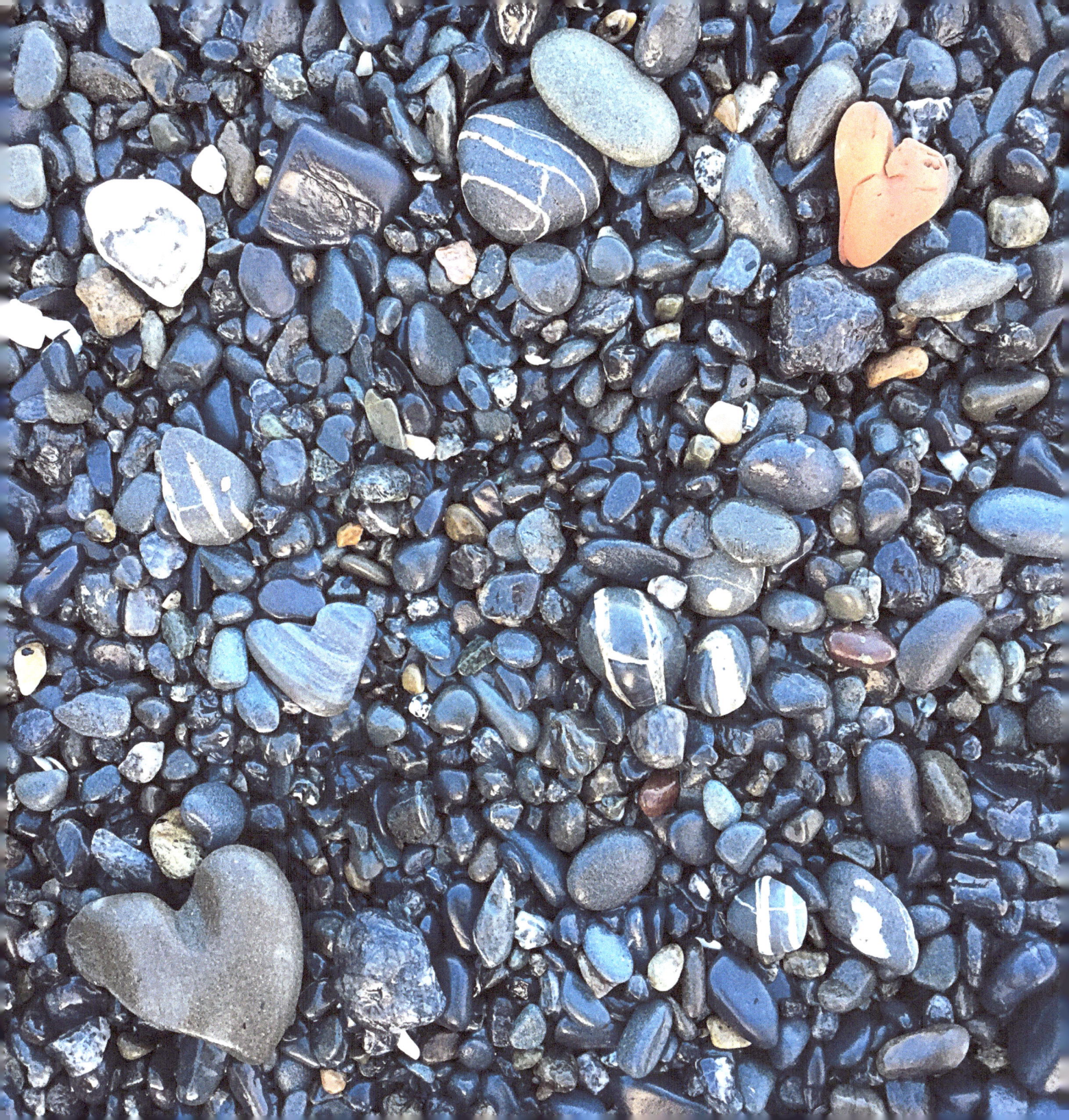

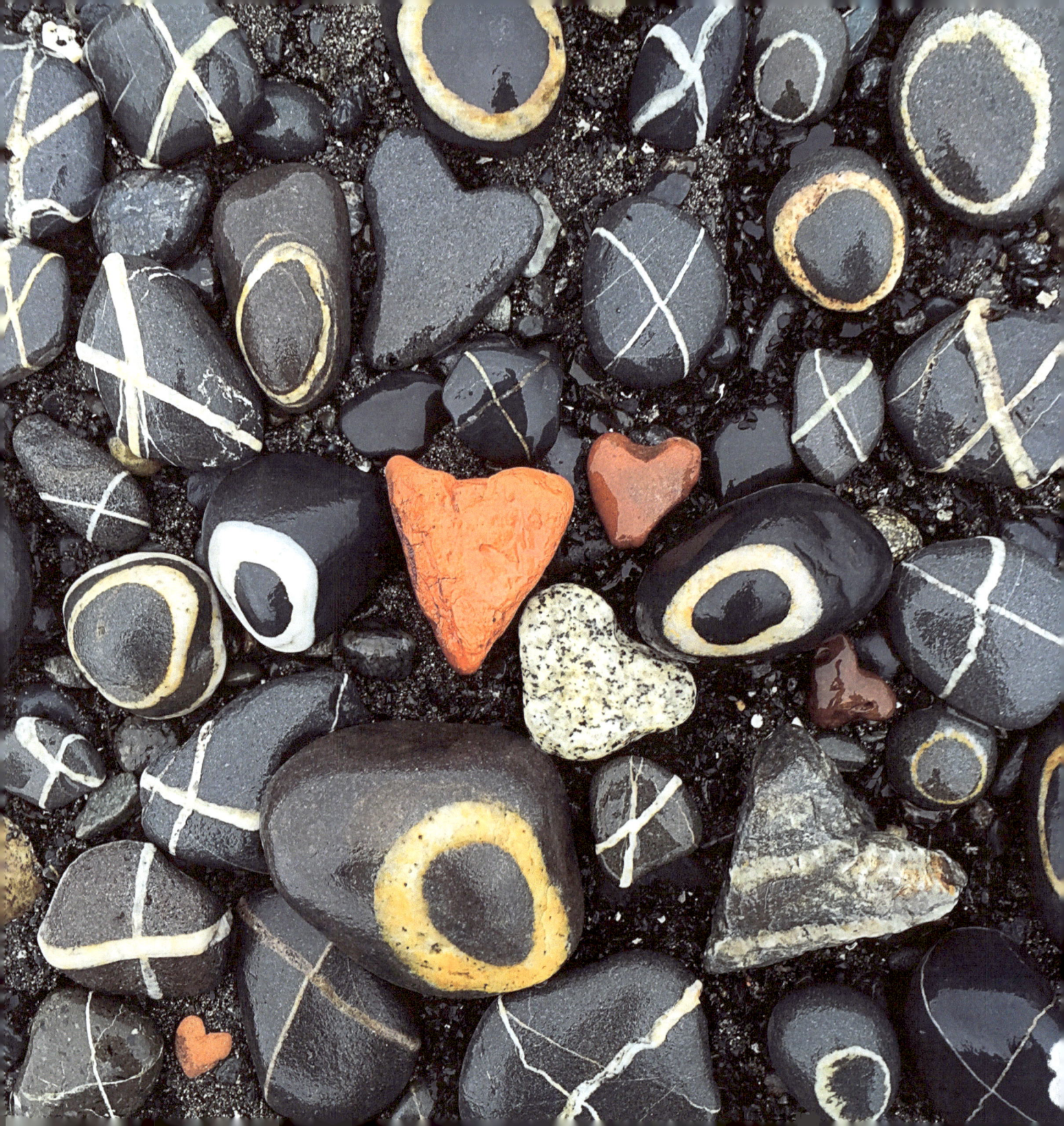

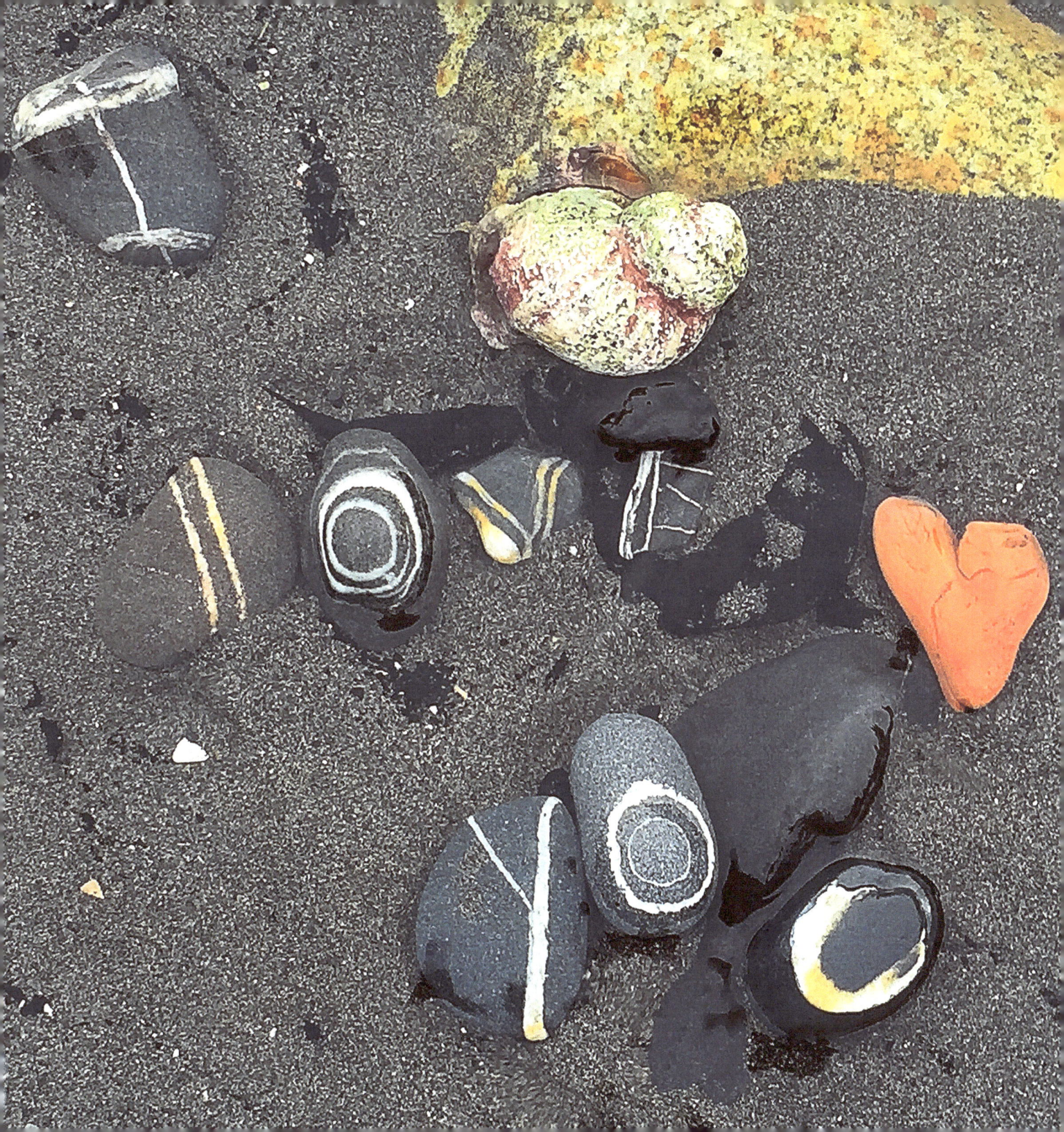

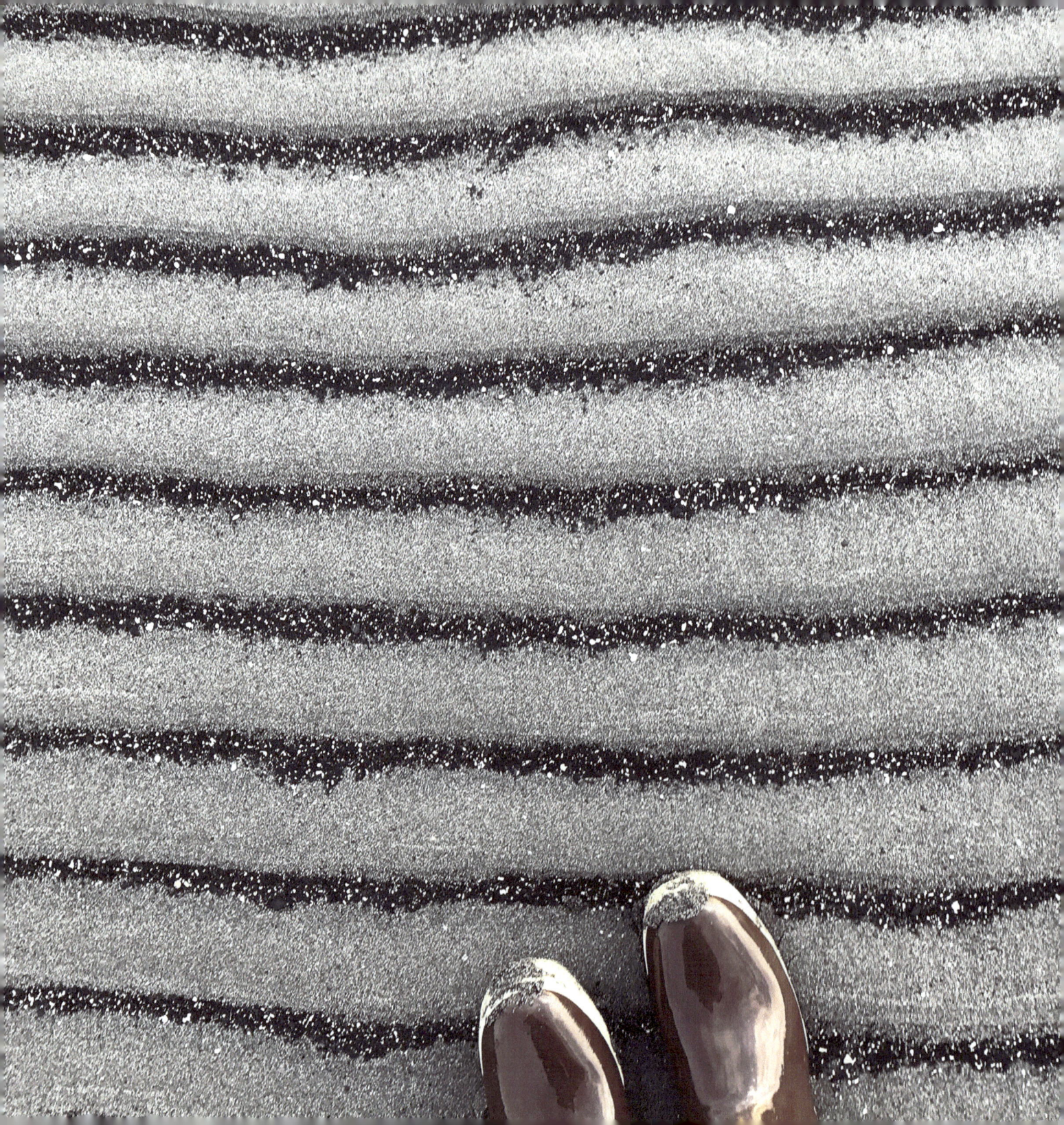

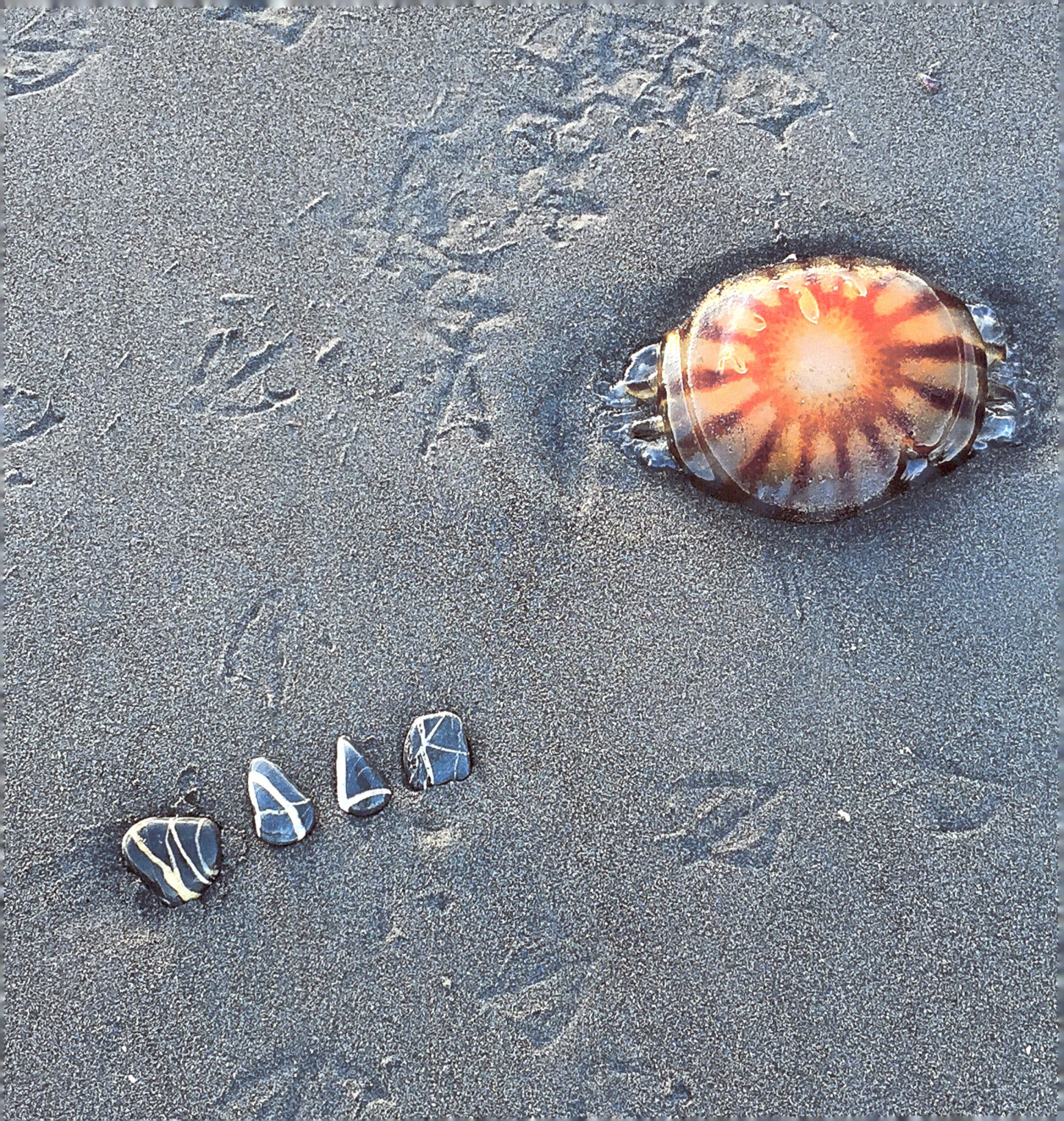

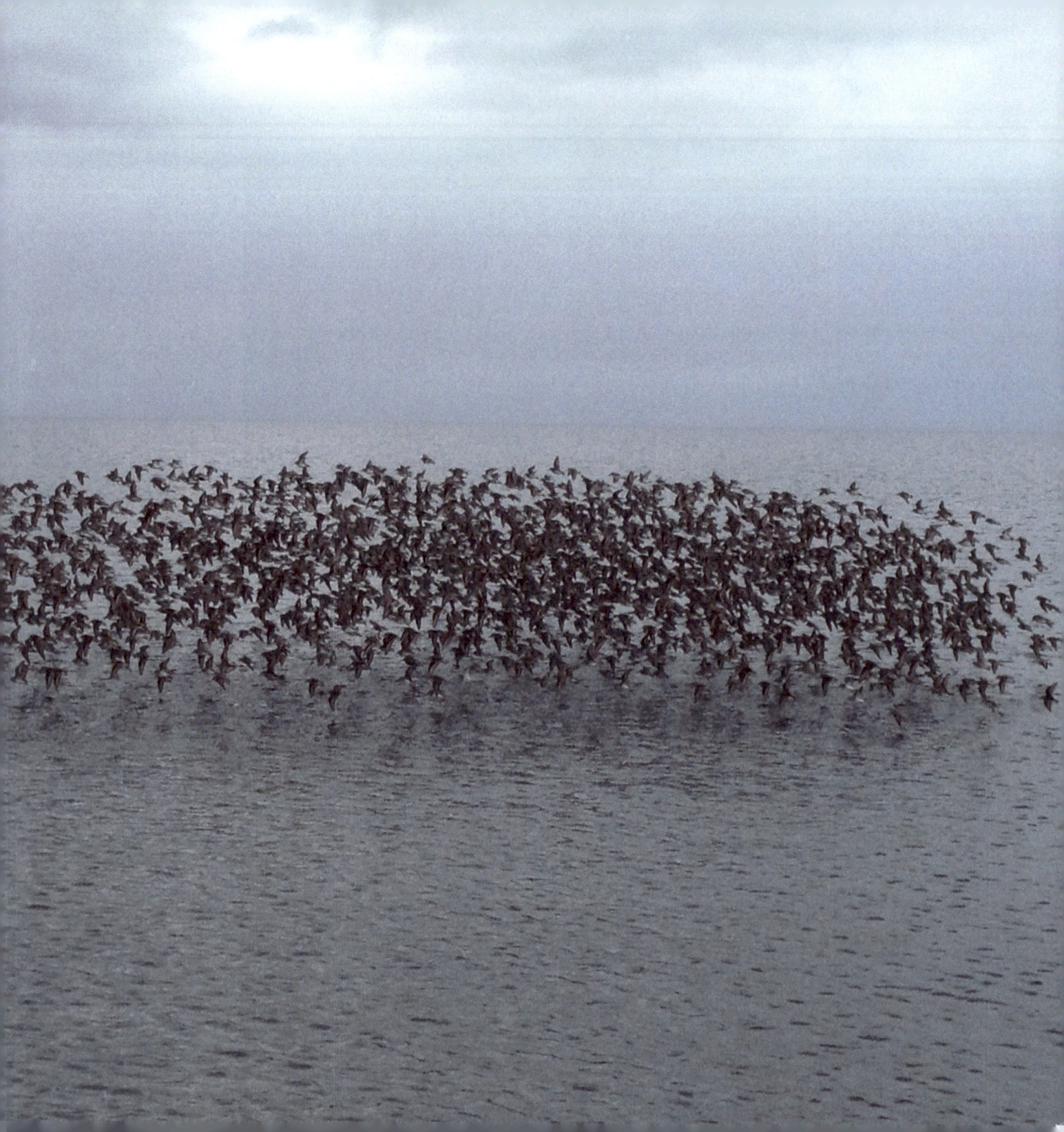

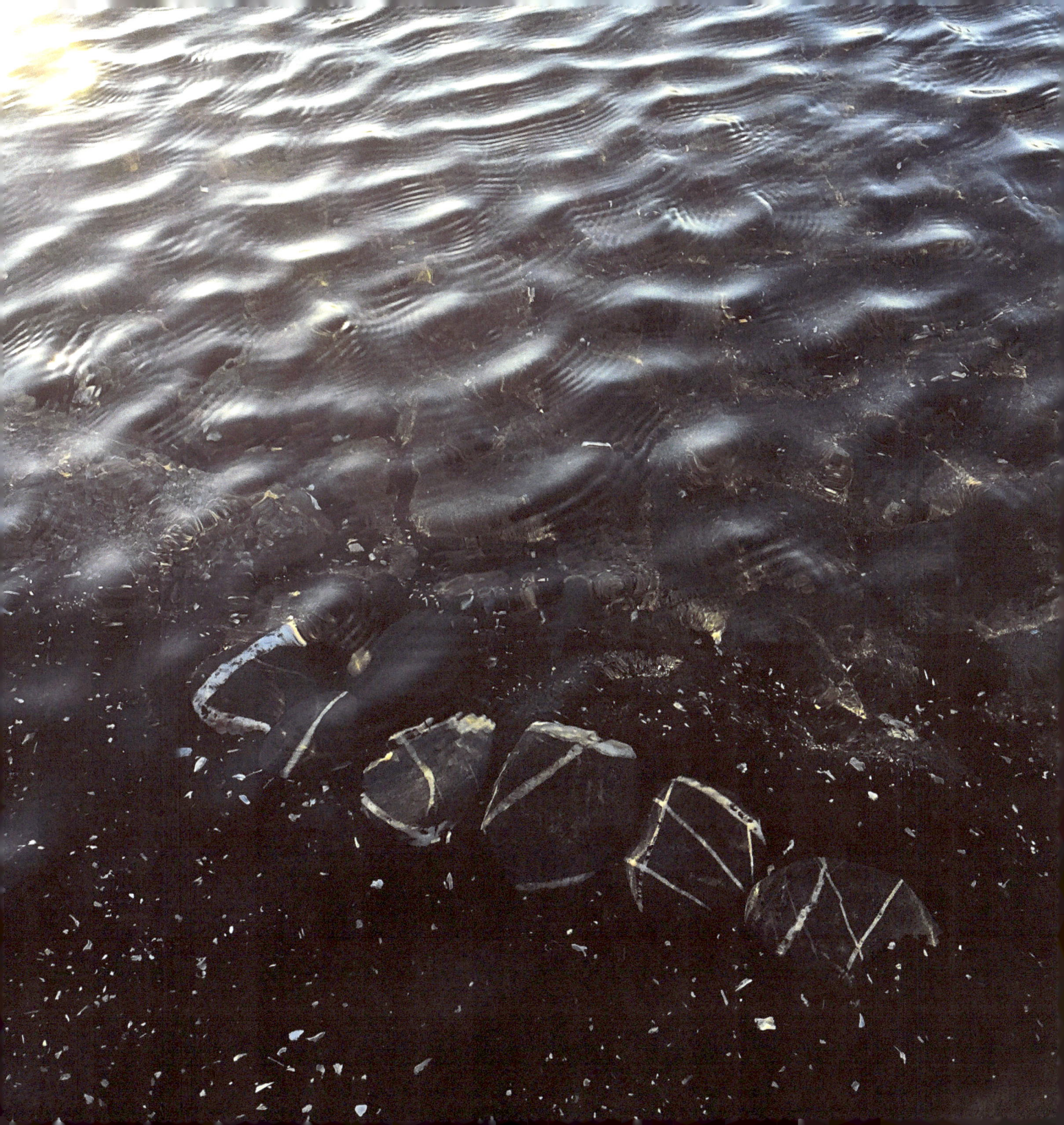

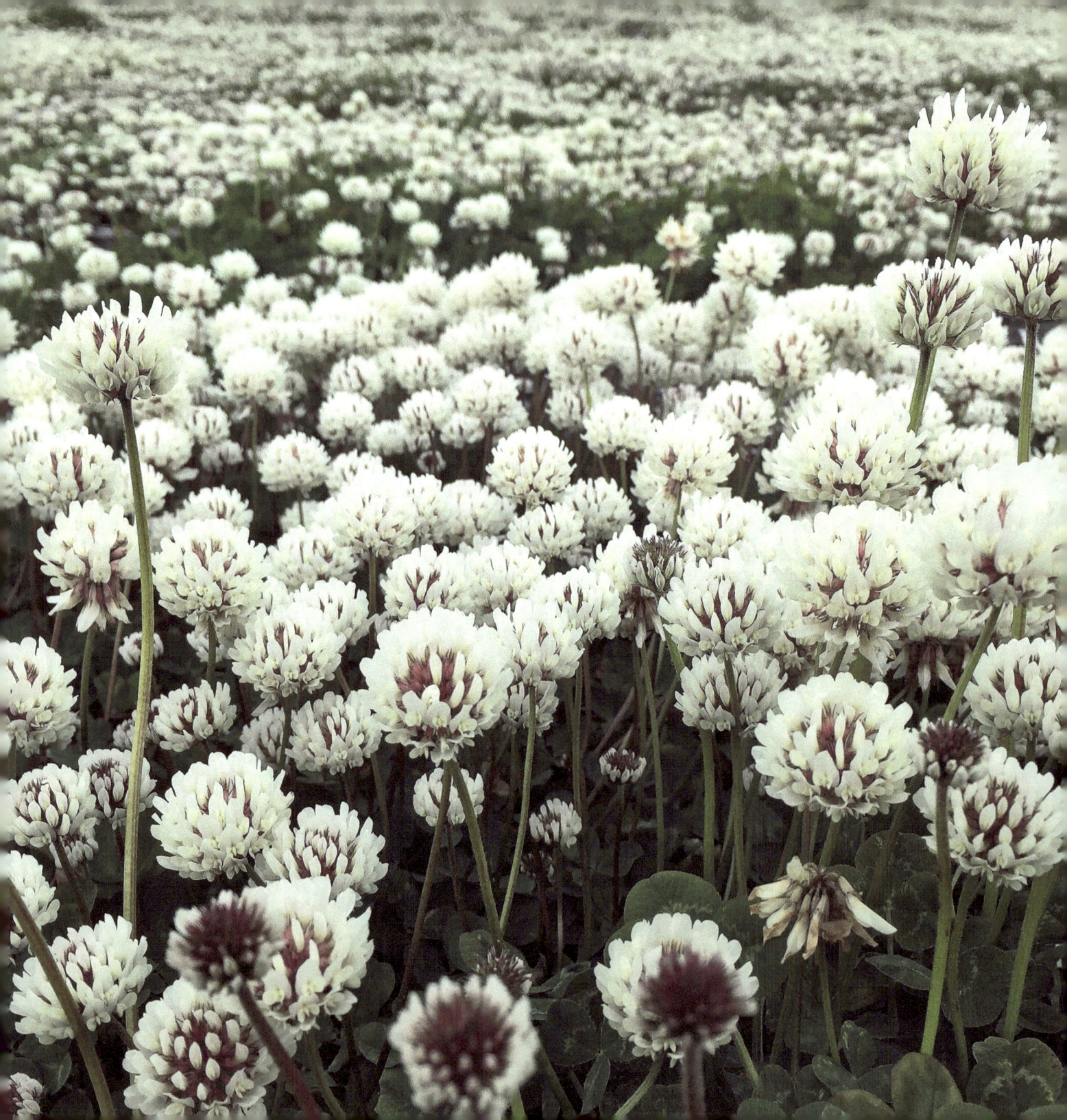

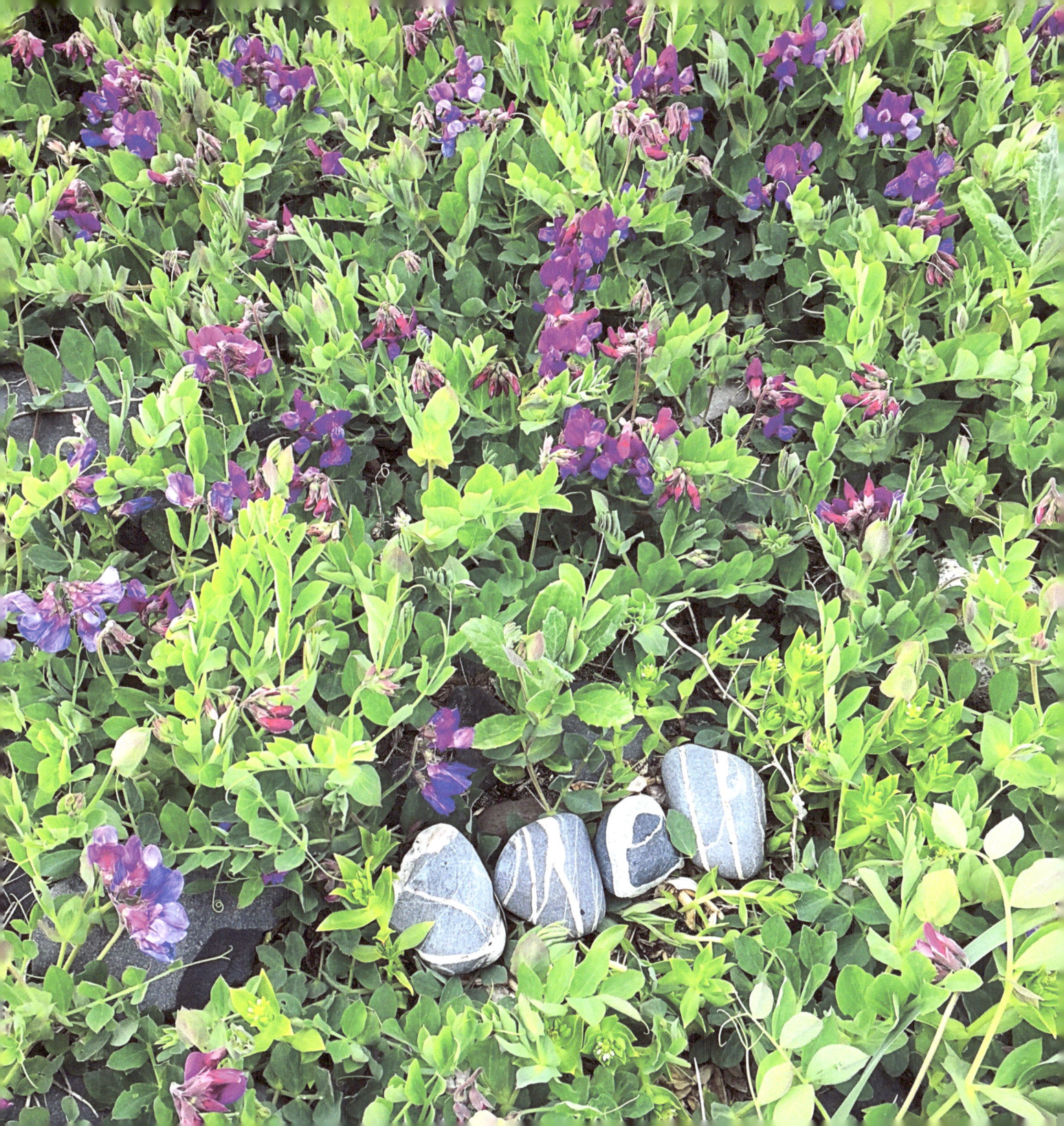

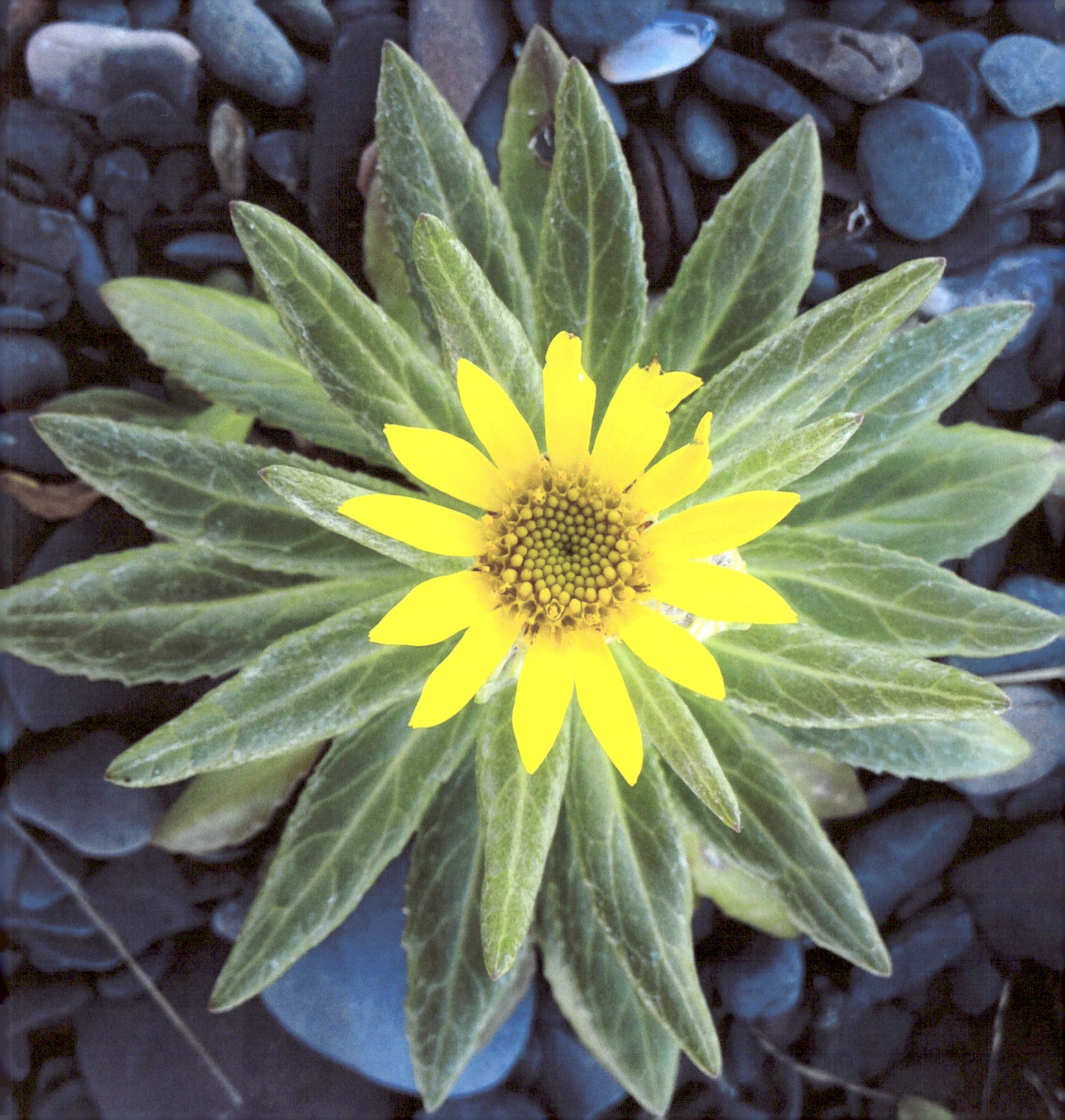

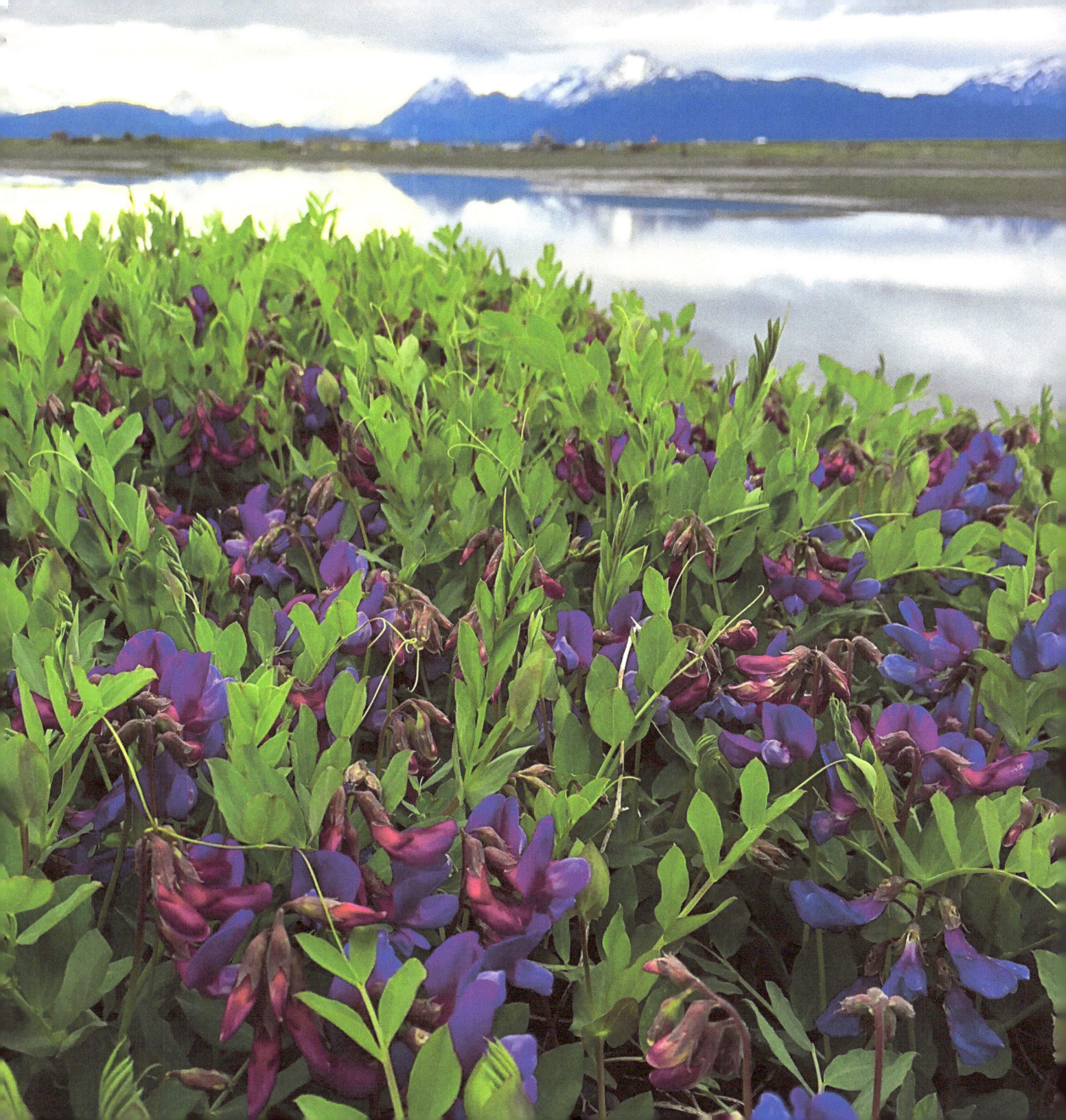

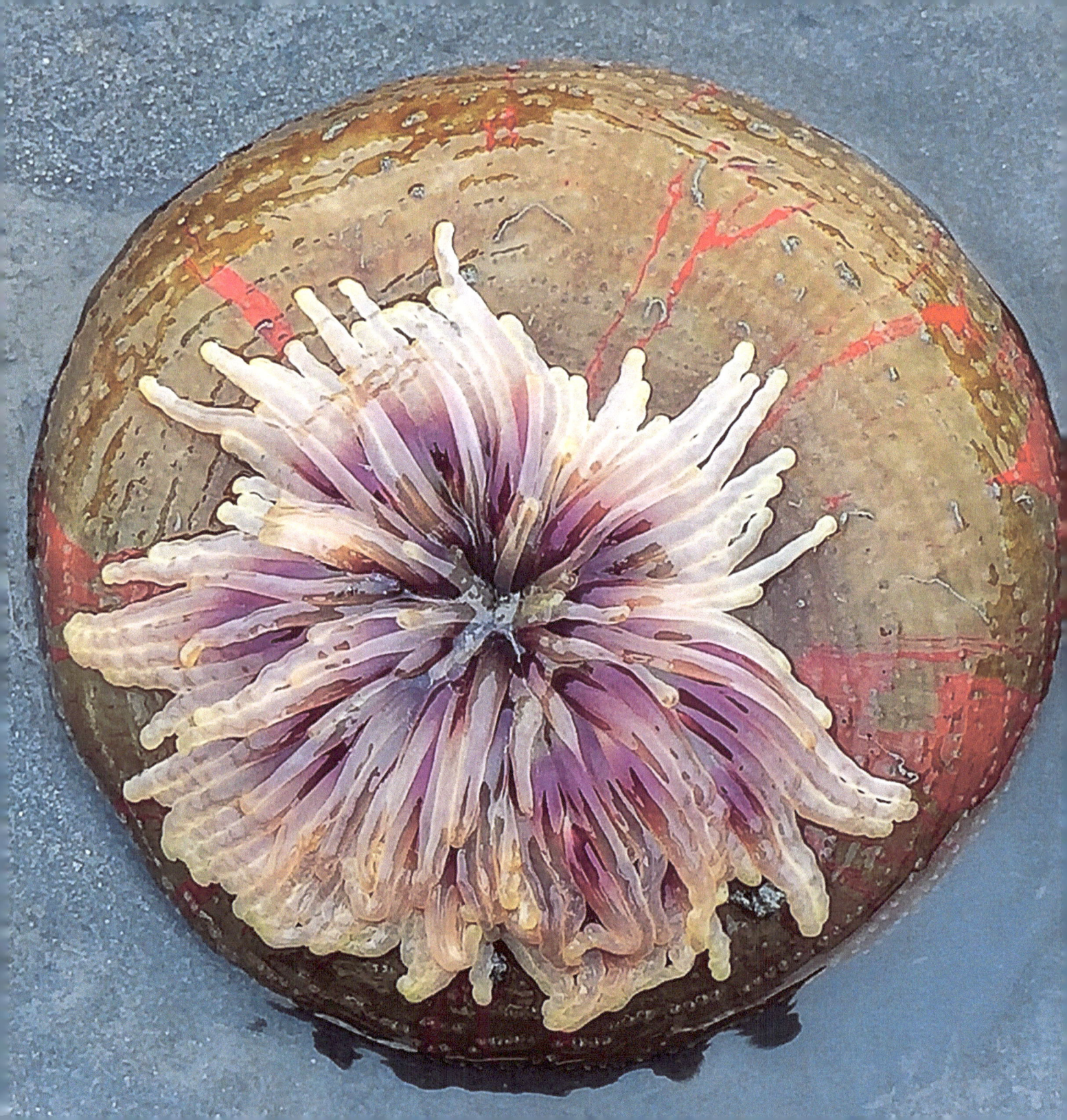

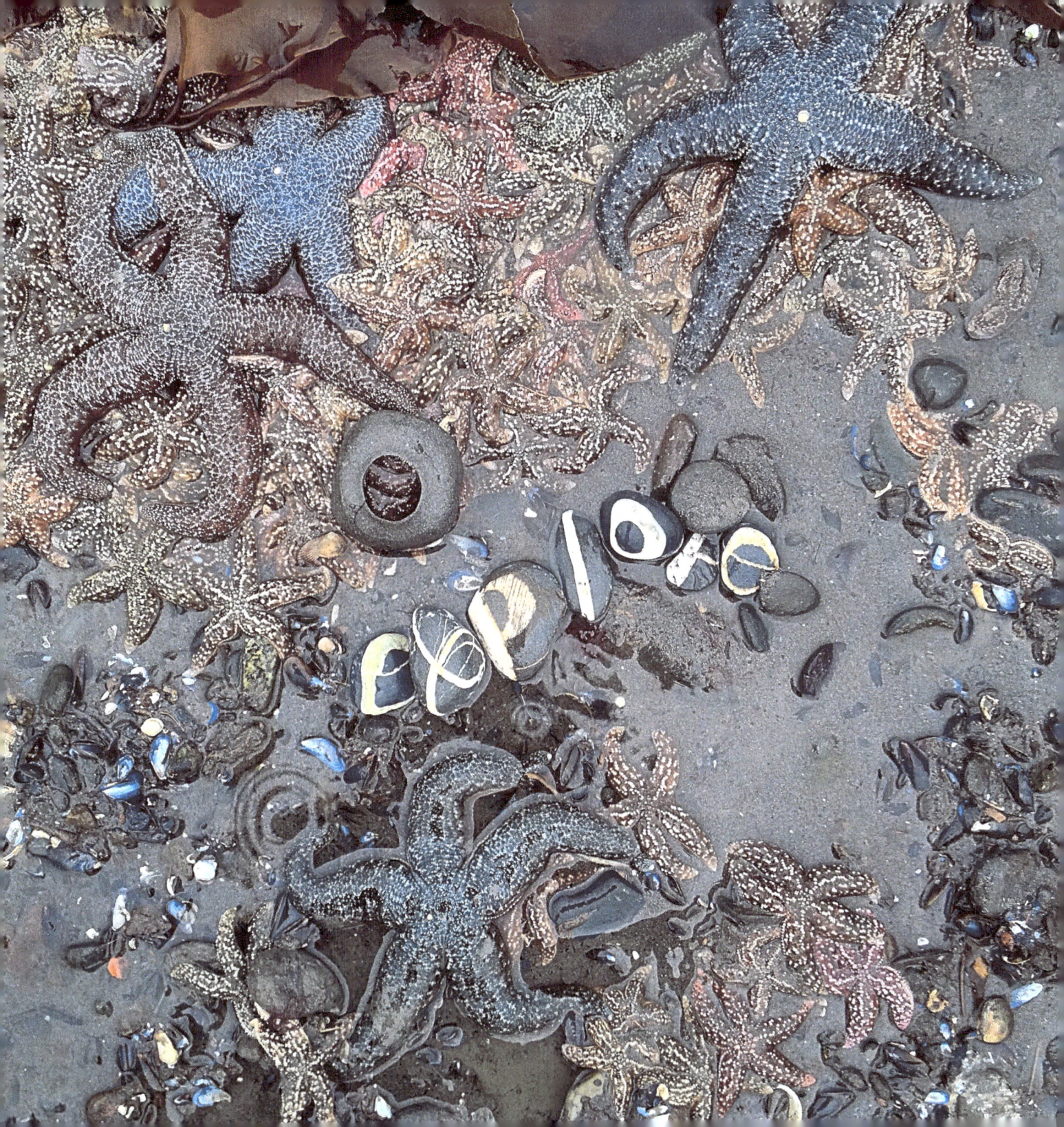

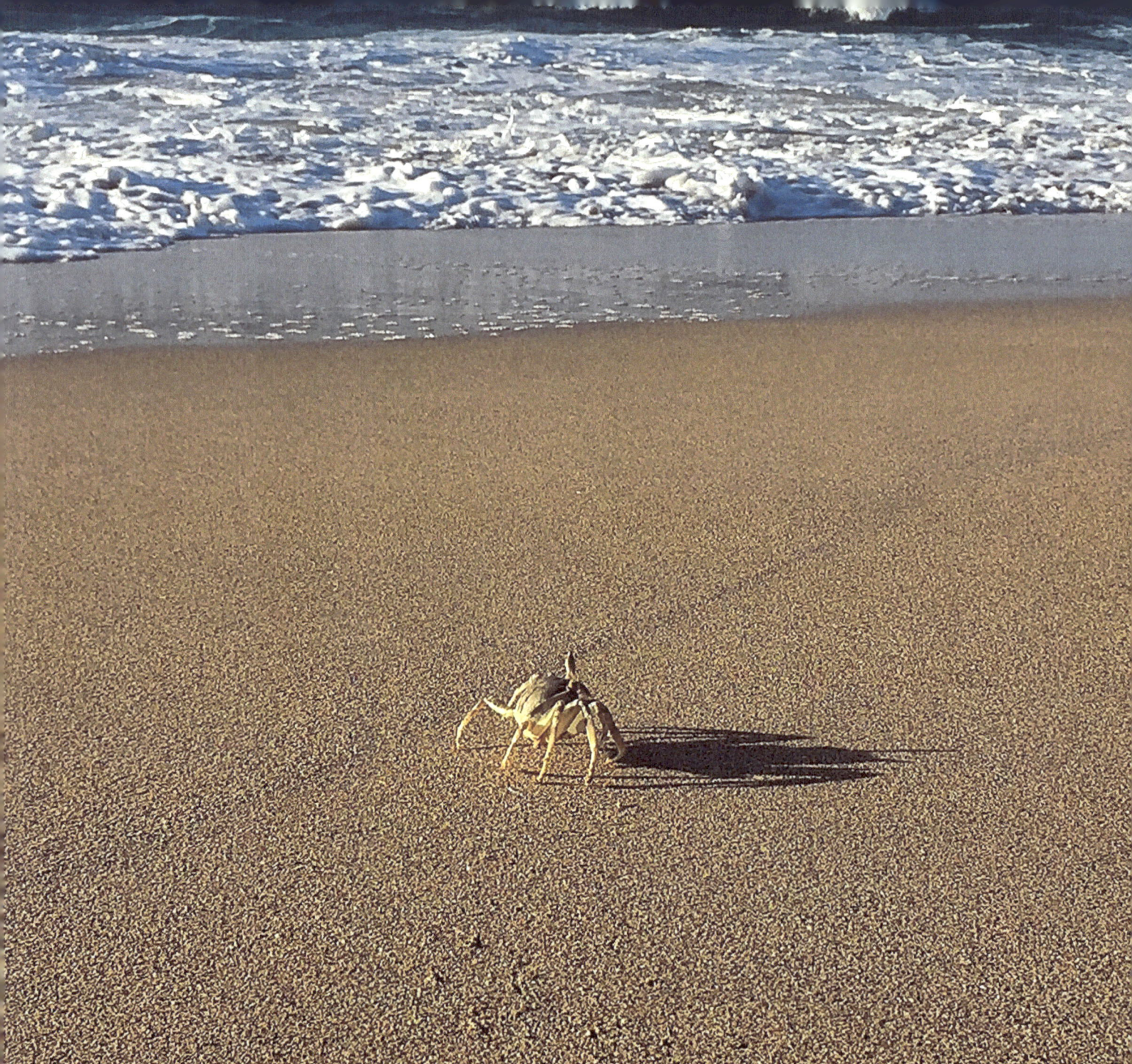

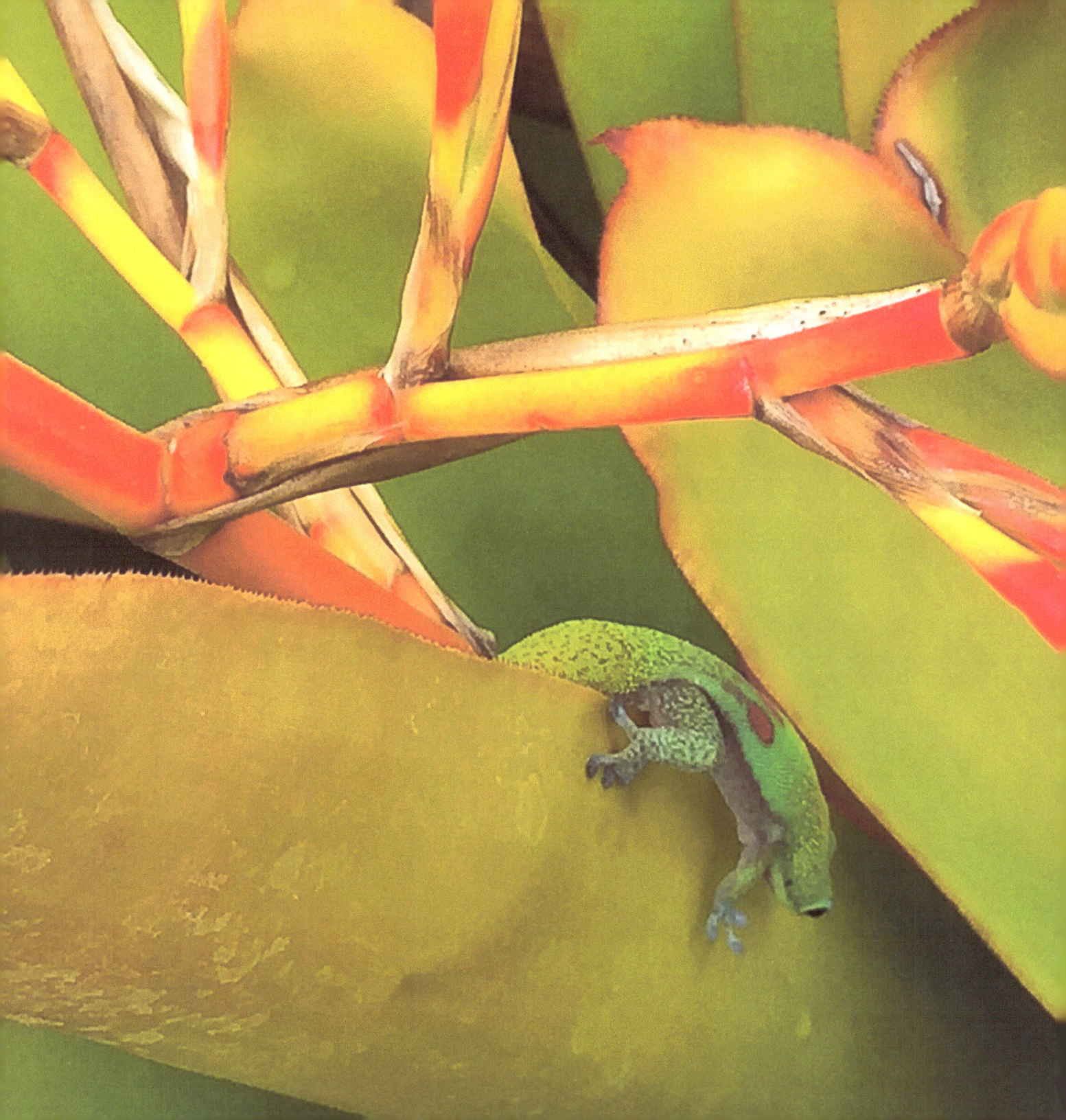

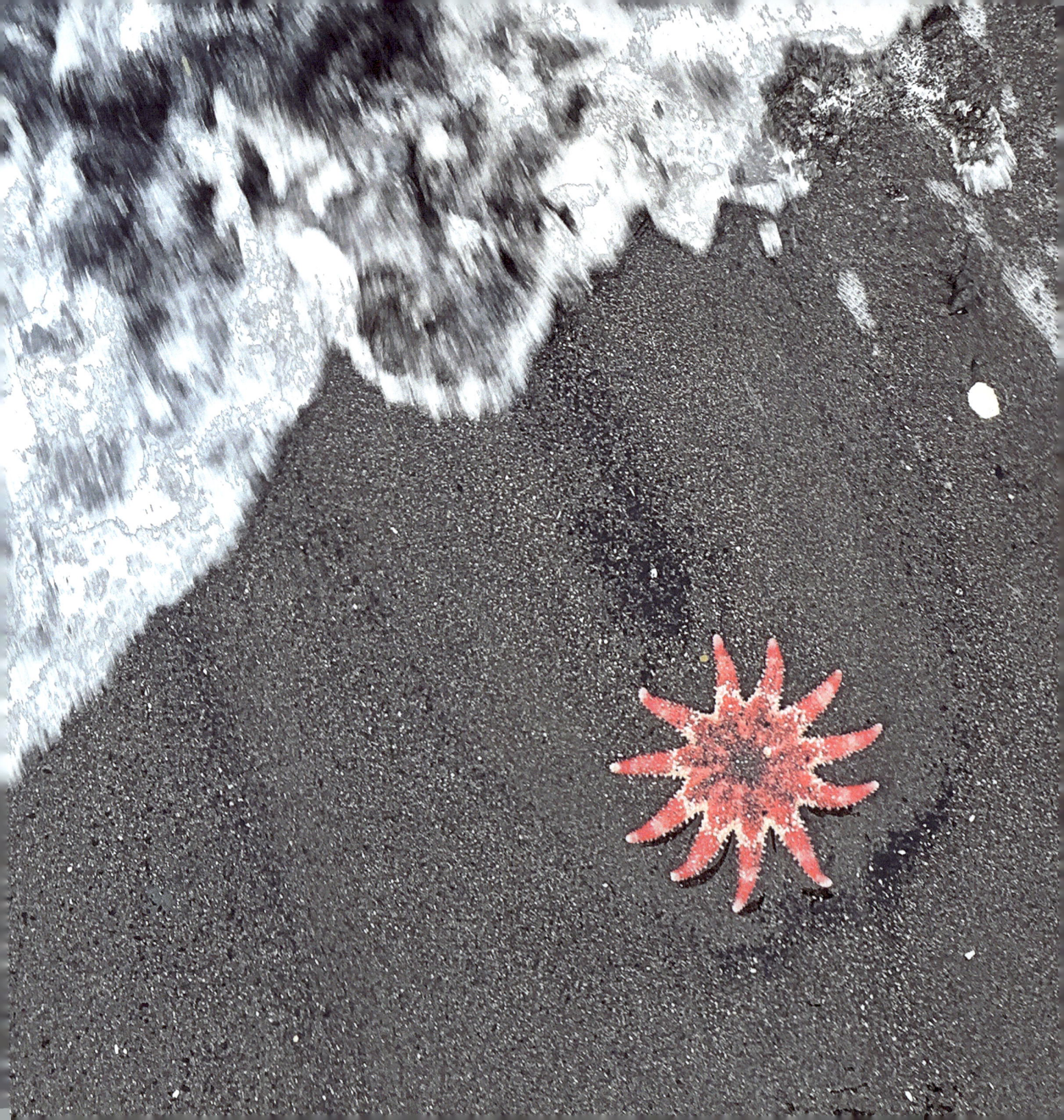

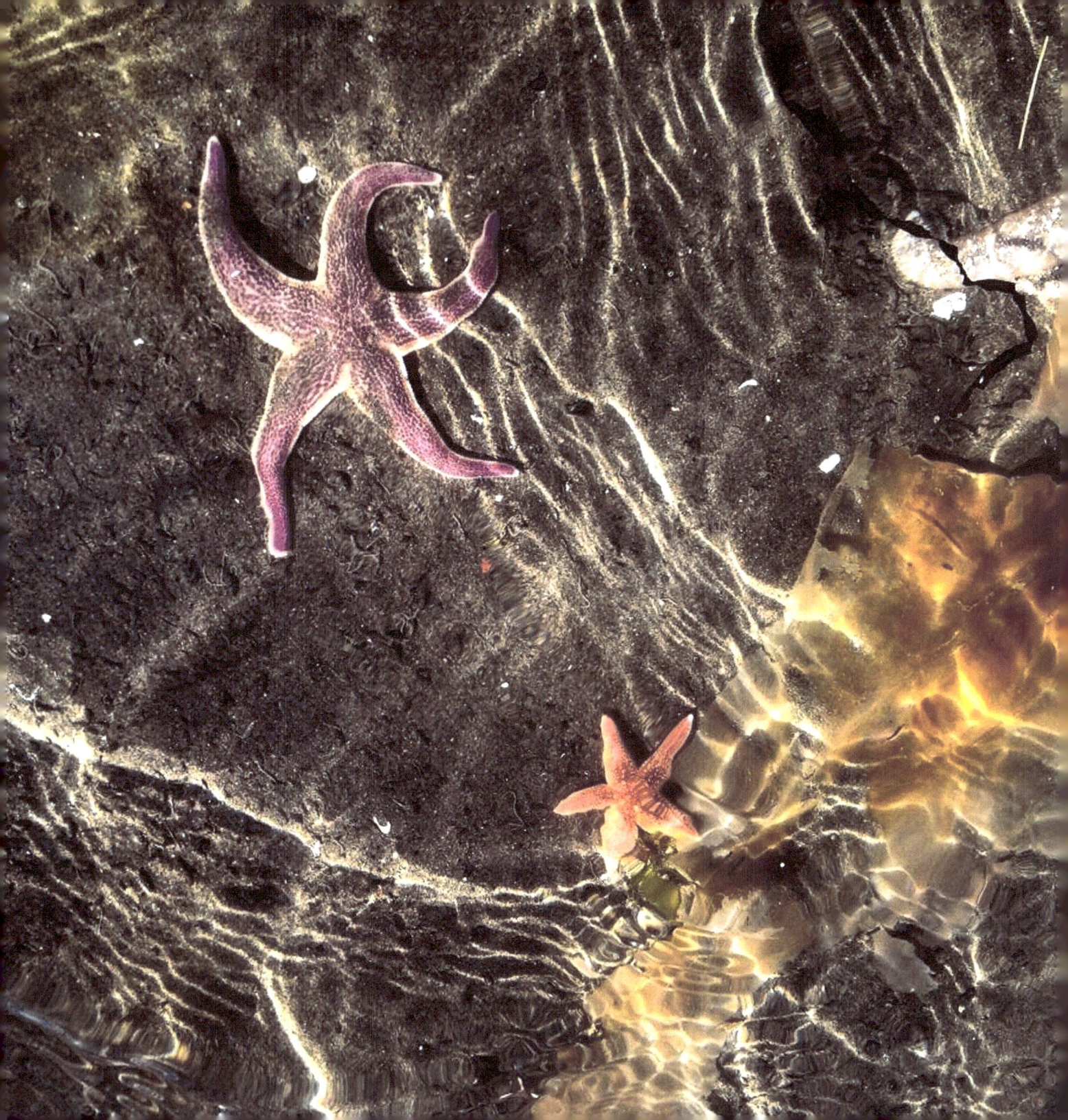

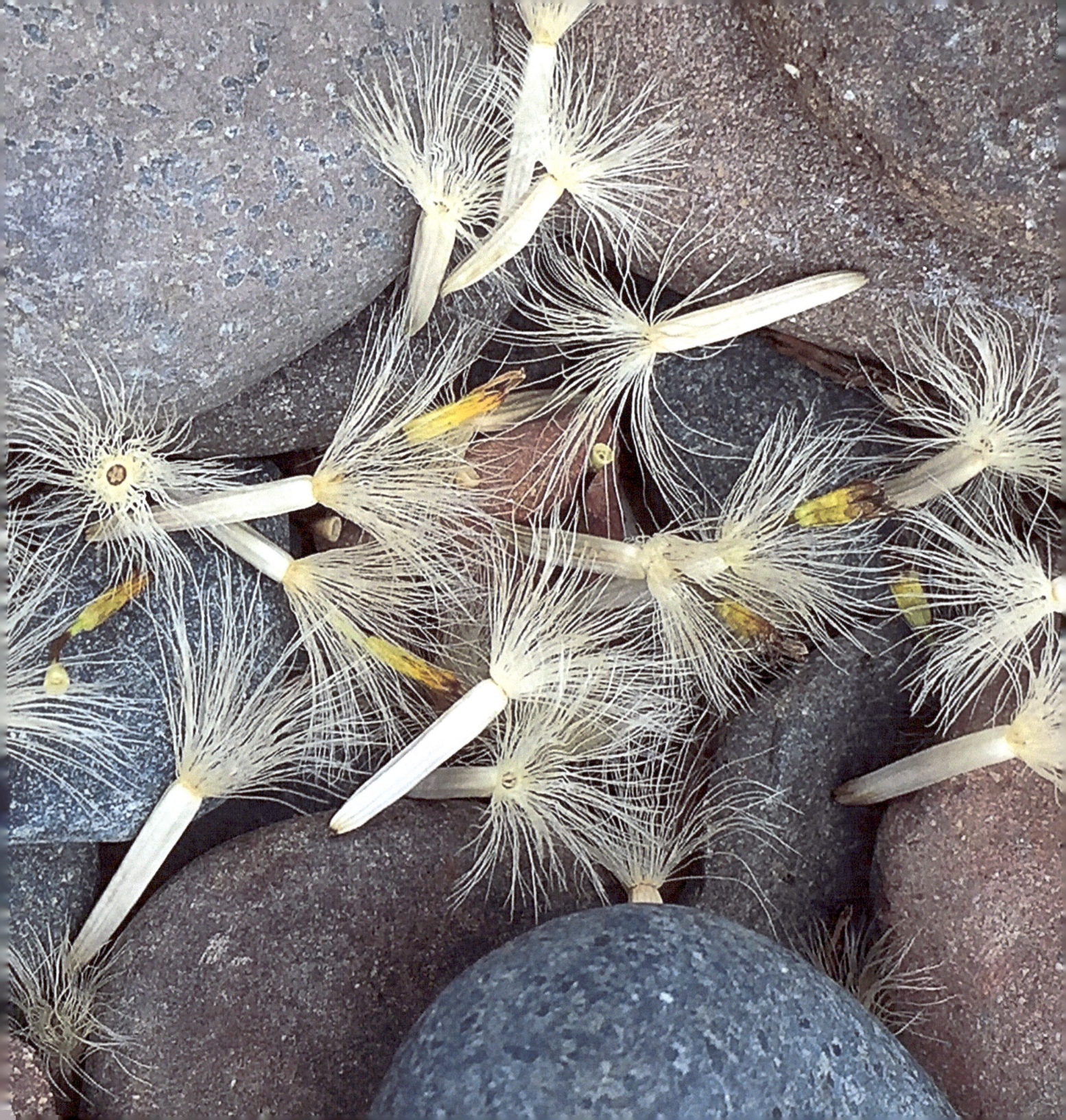

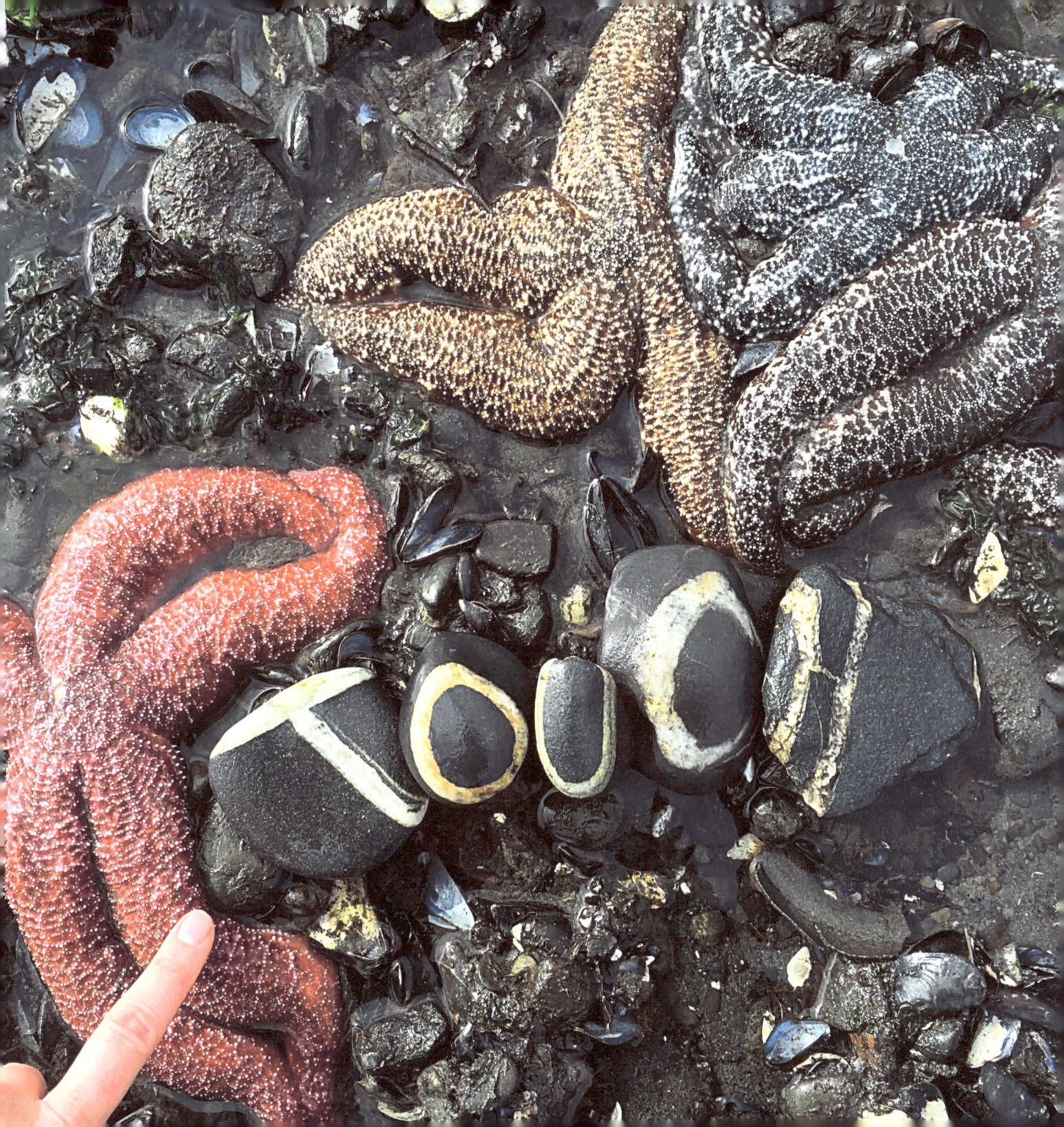

Aa Bb Cc Dd
Ee Ff Gg Hh Ii
Jj Kk Ll Mm
Nn Oo Pp Qq
Rr Ss Tt Uu
Vv Ww Xx Yy
Zz

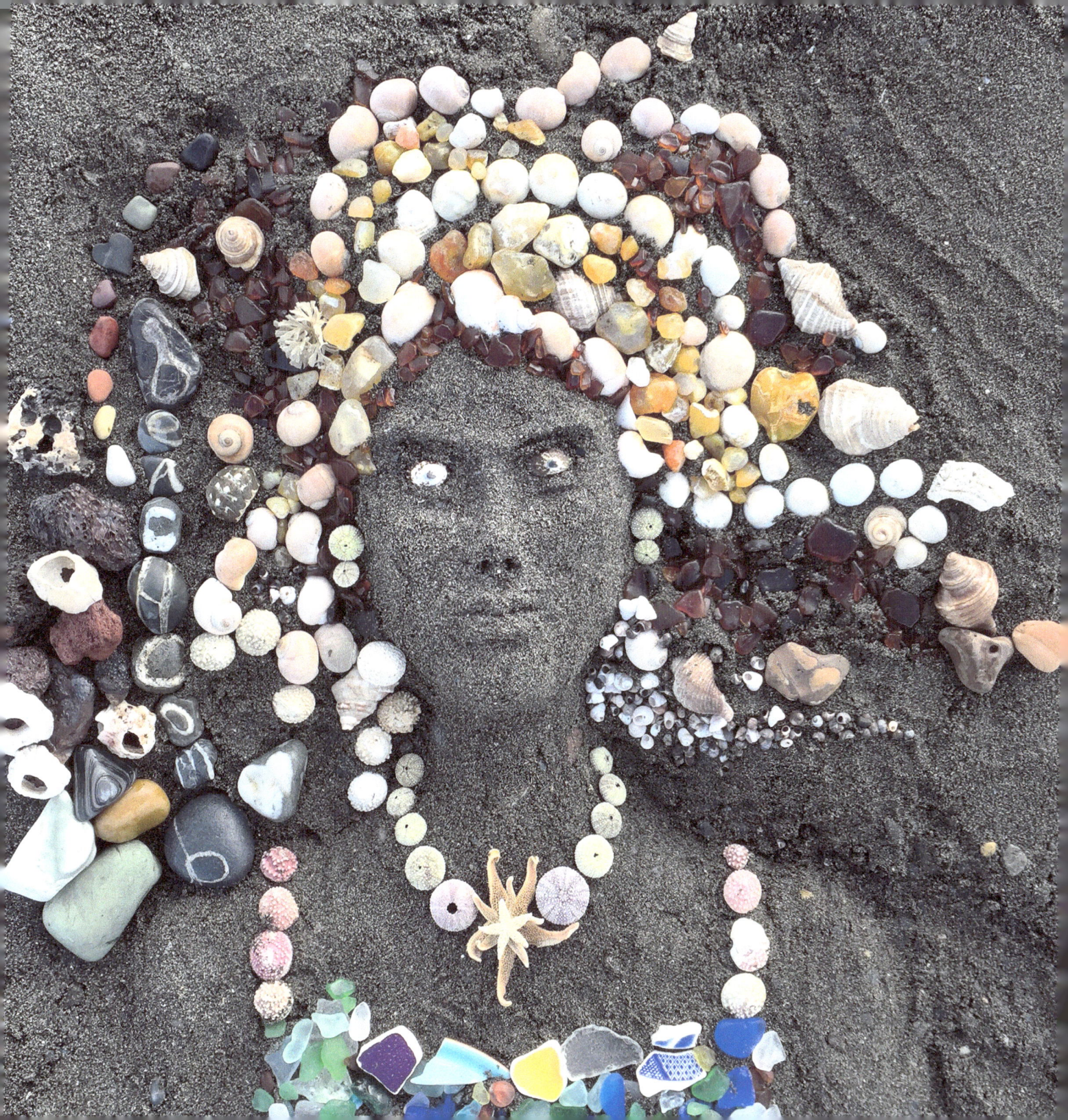

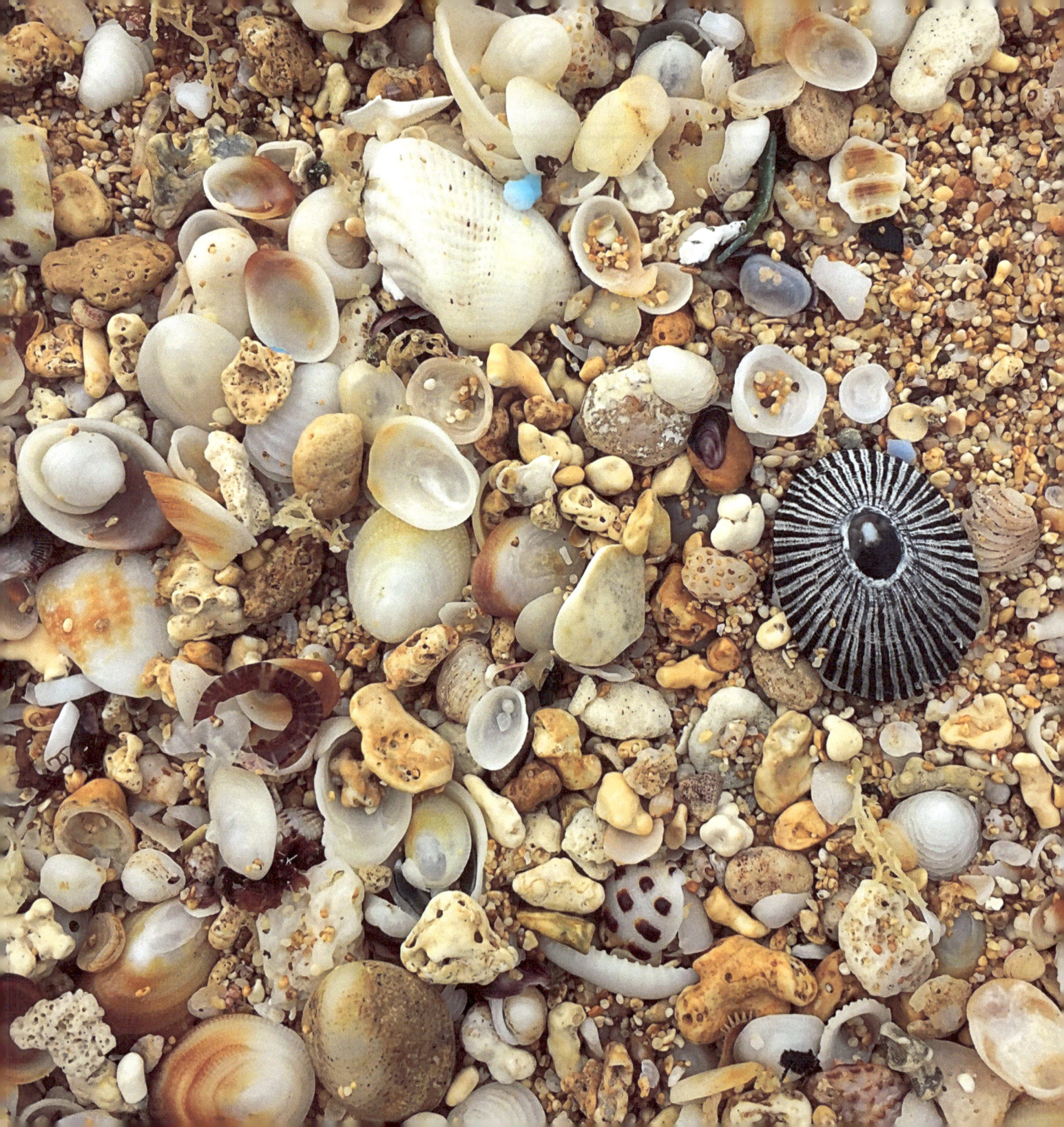

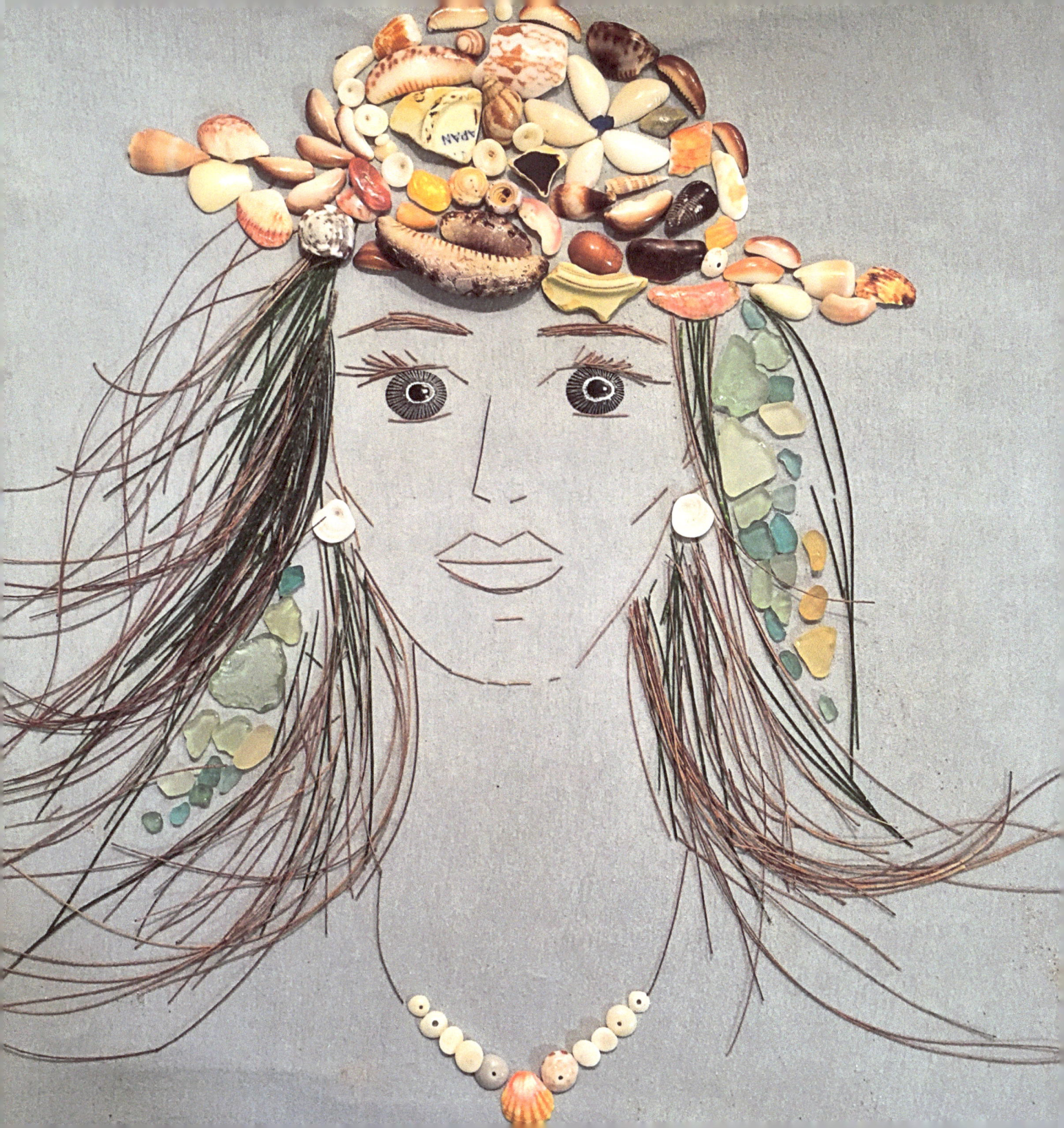

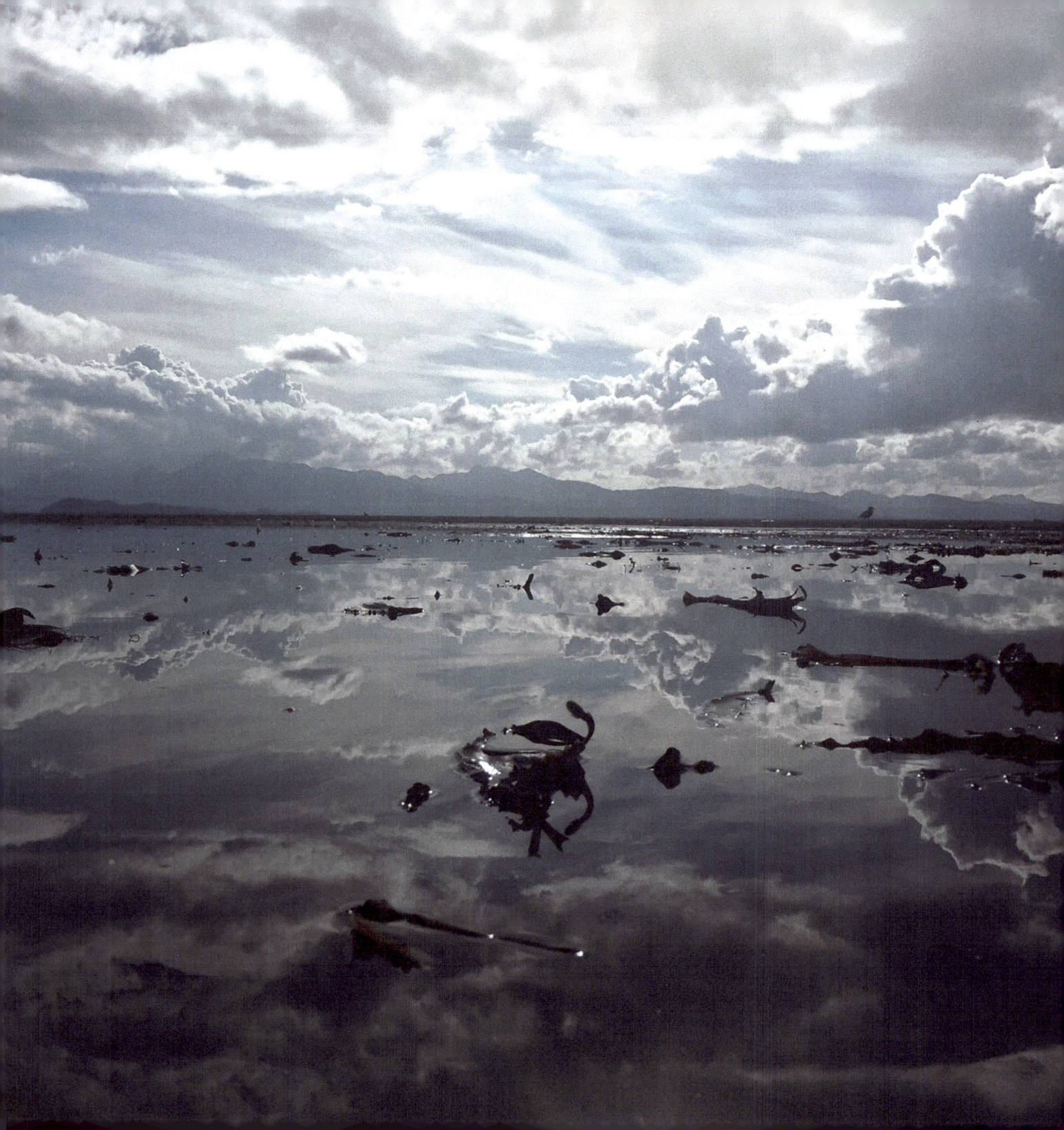

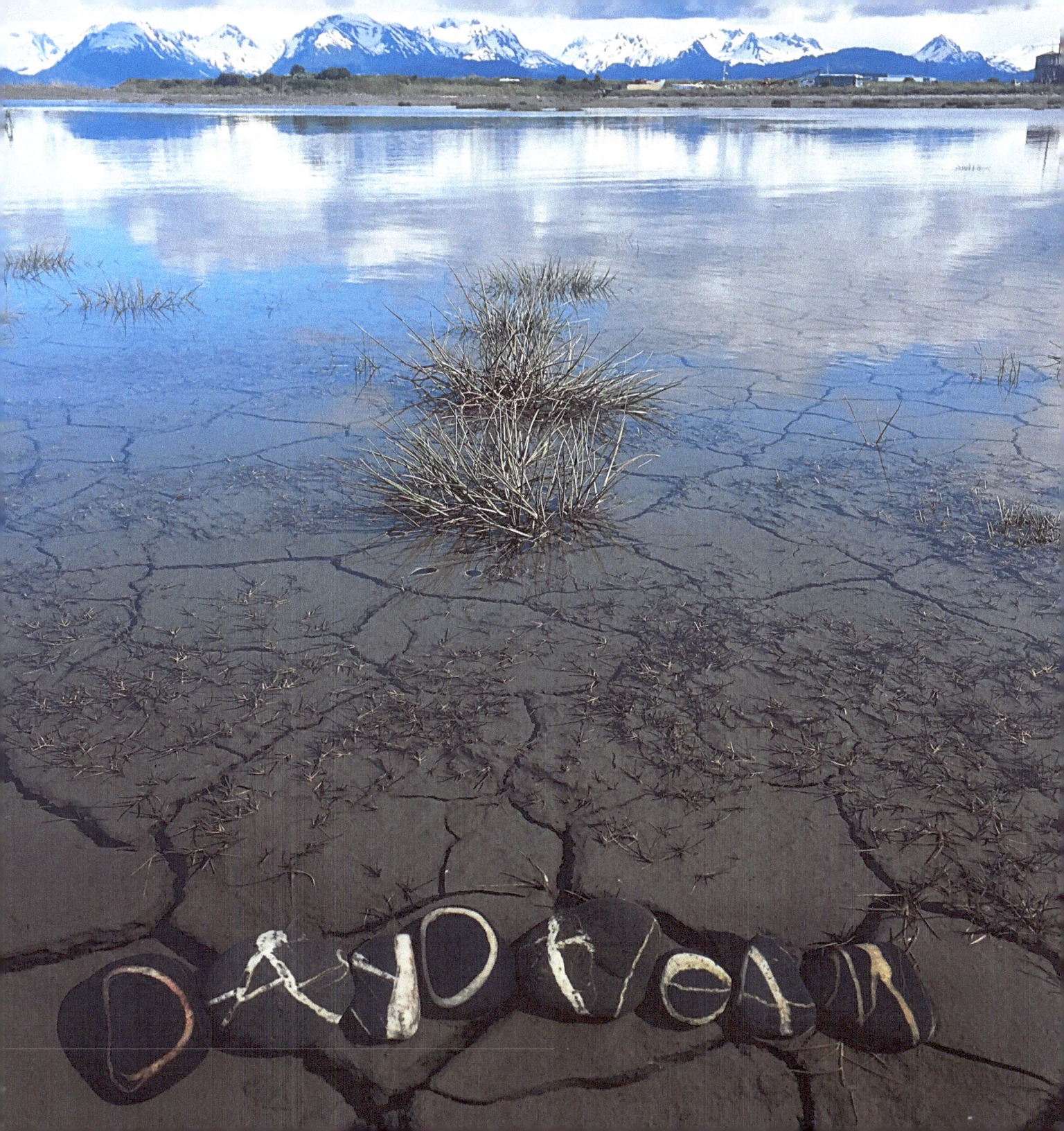

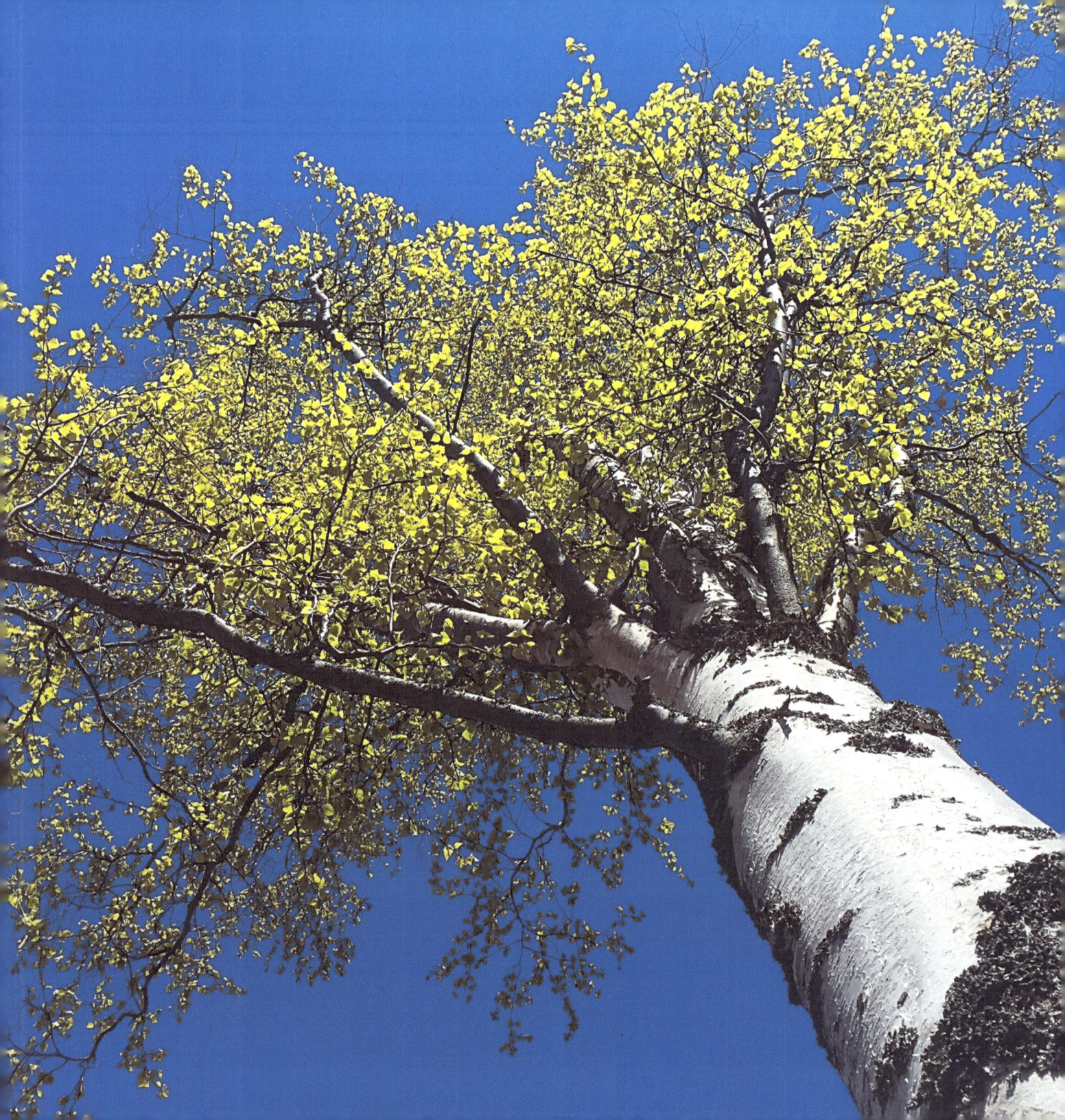

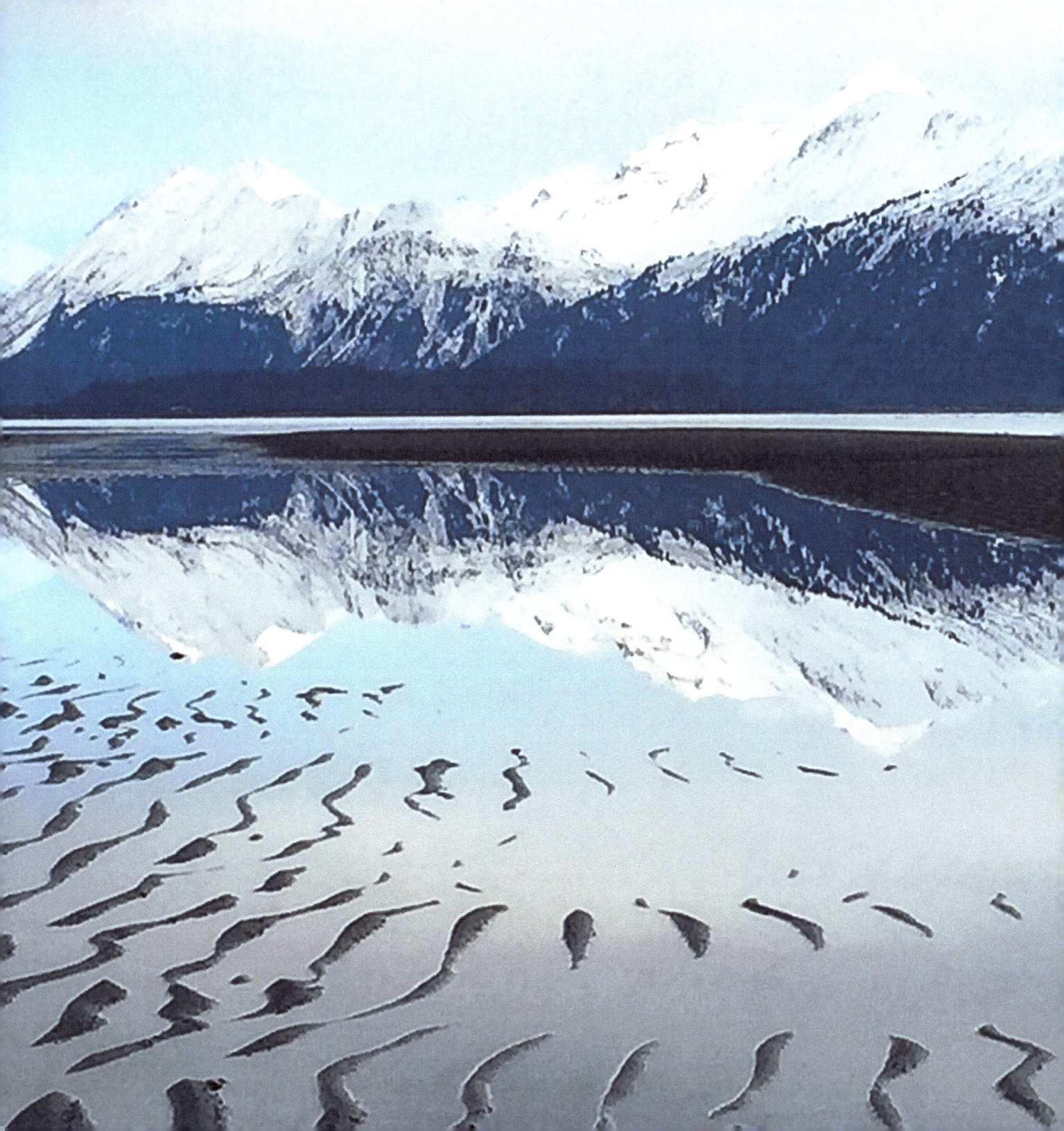

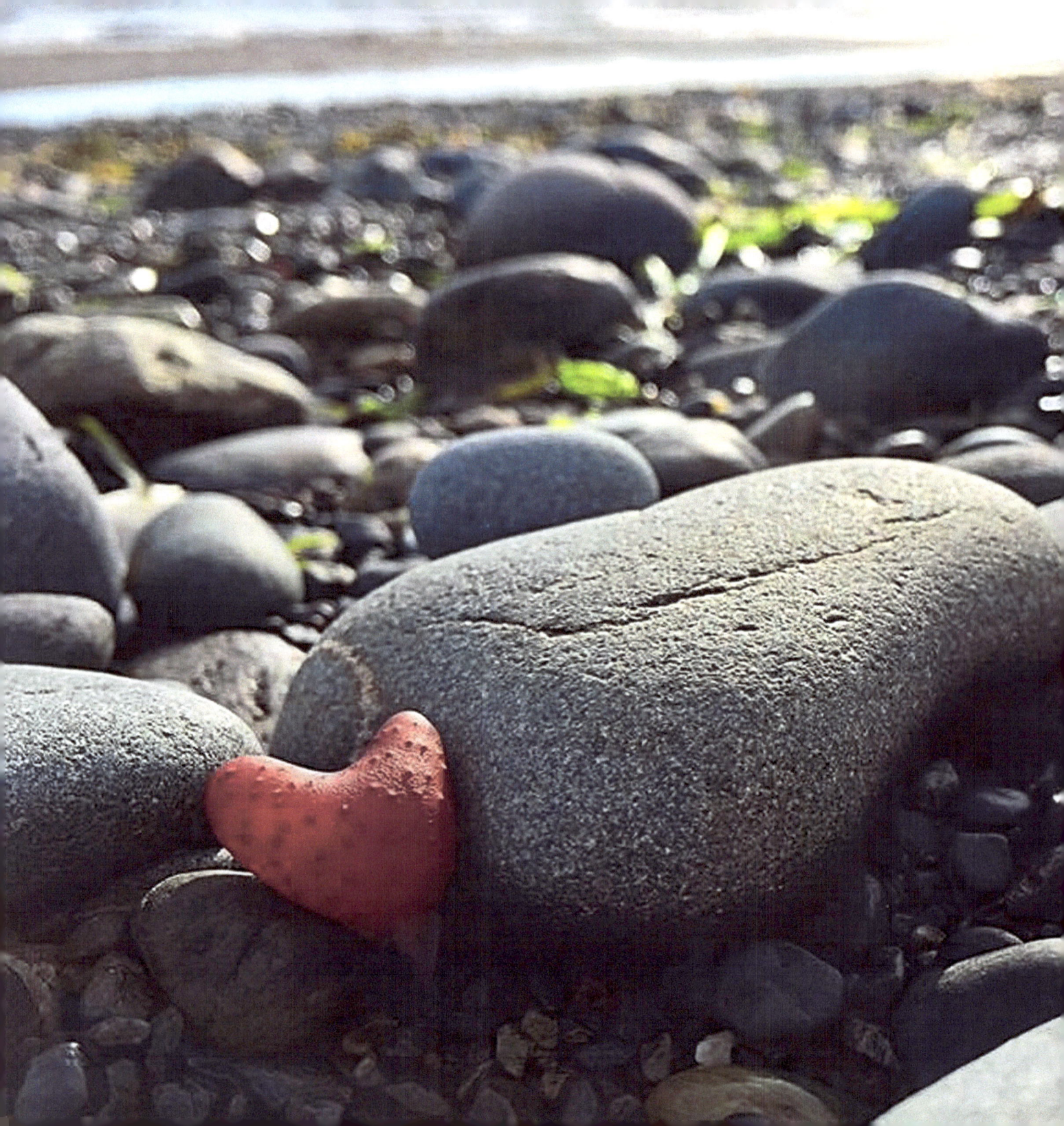

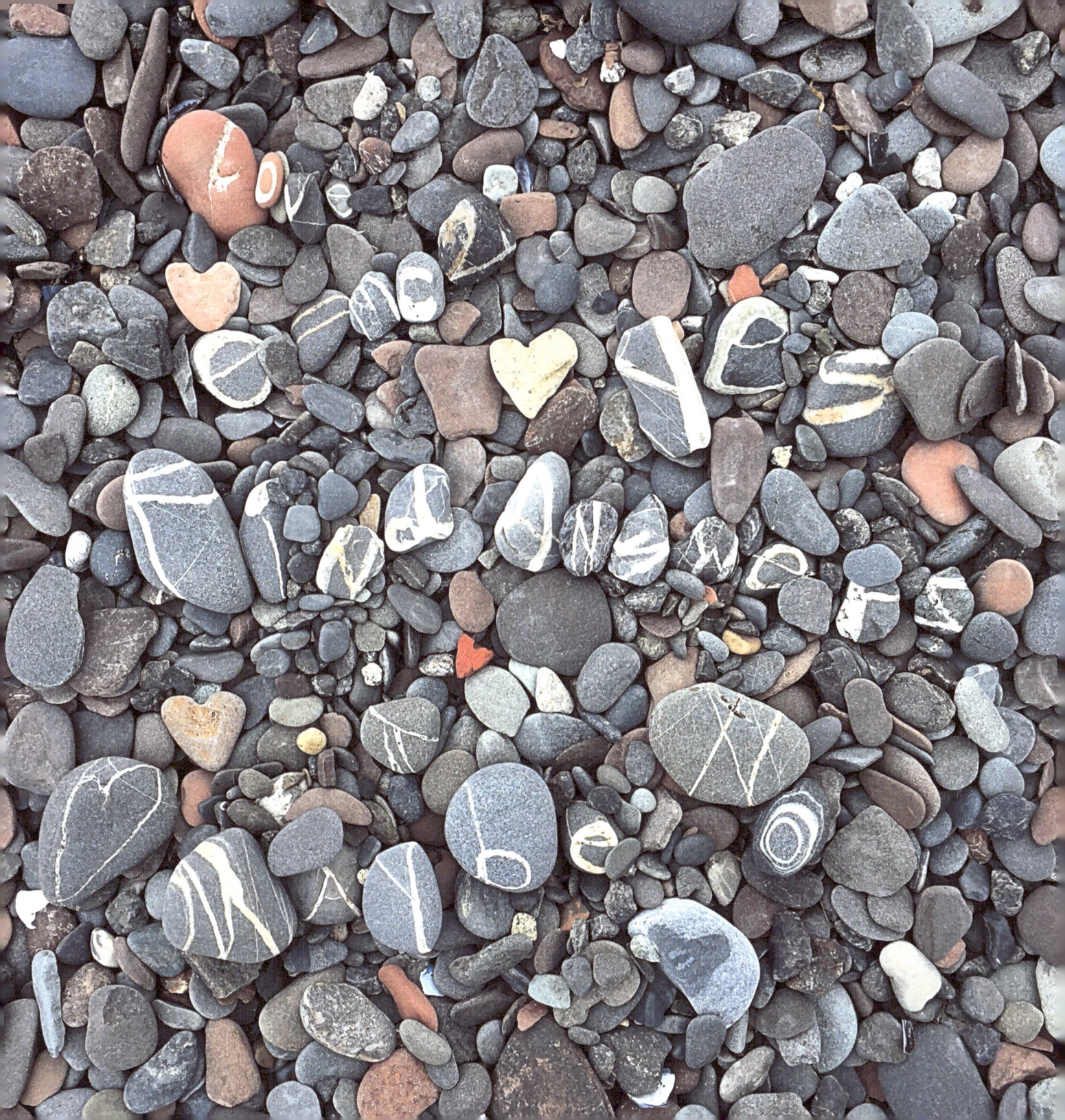

It was a dark and stormy night.

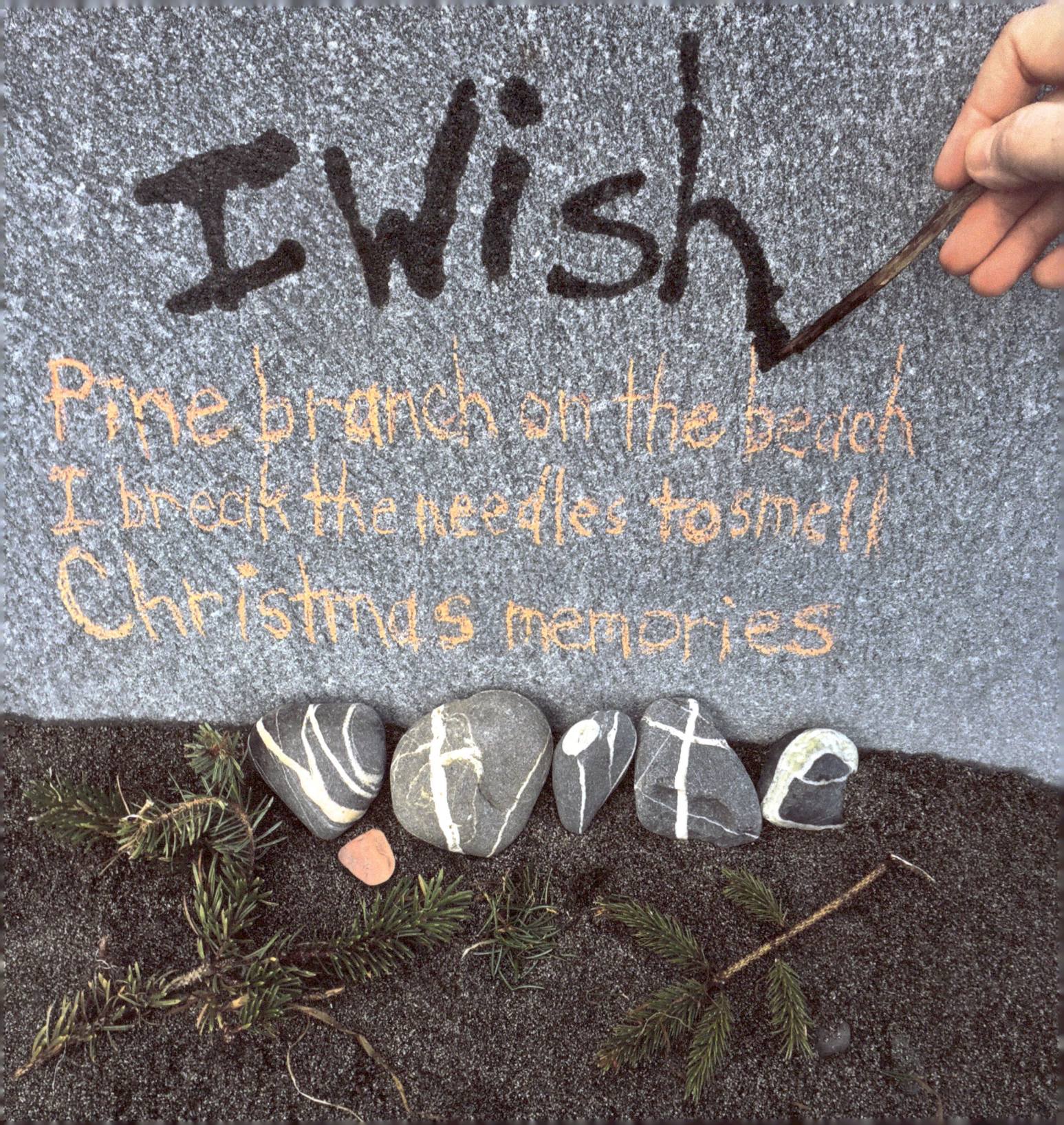

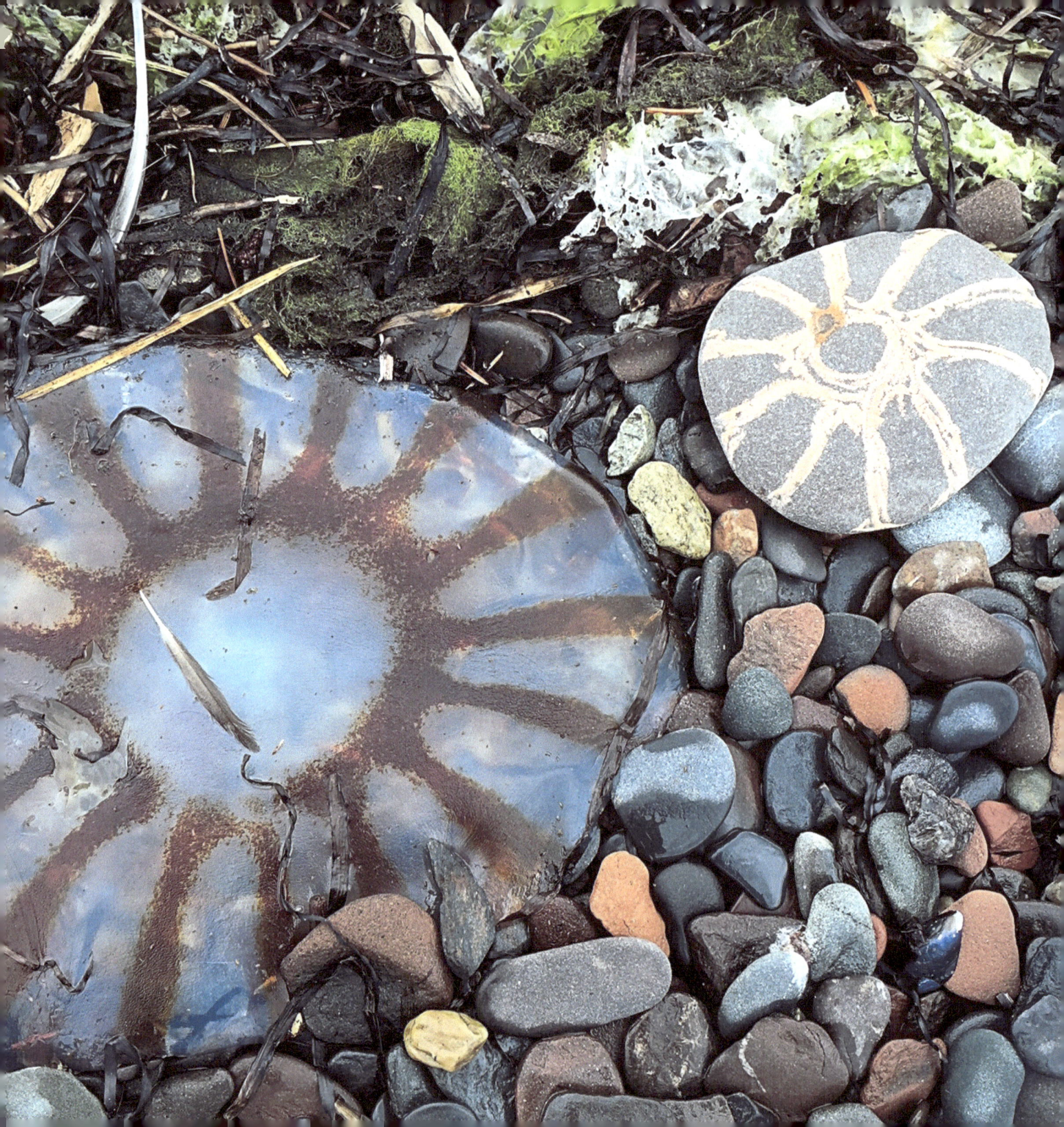

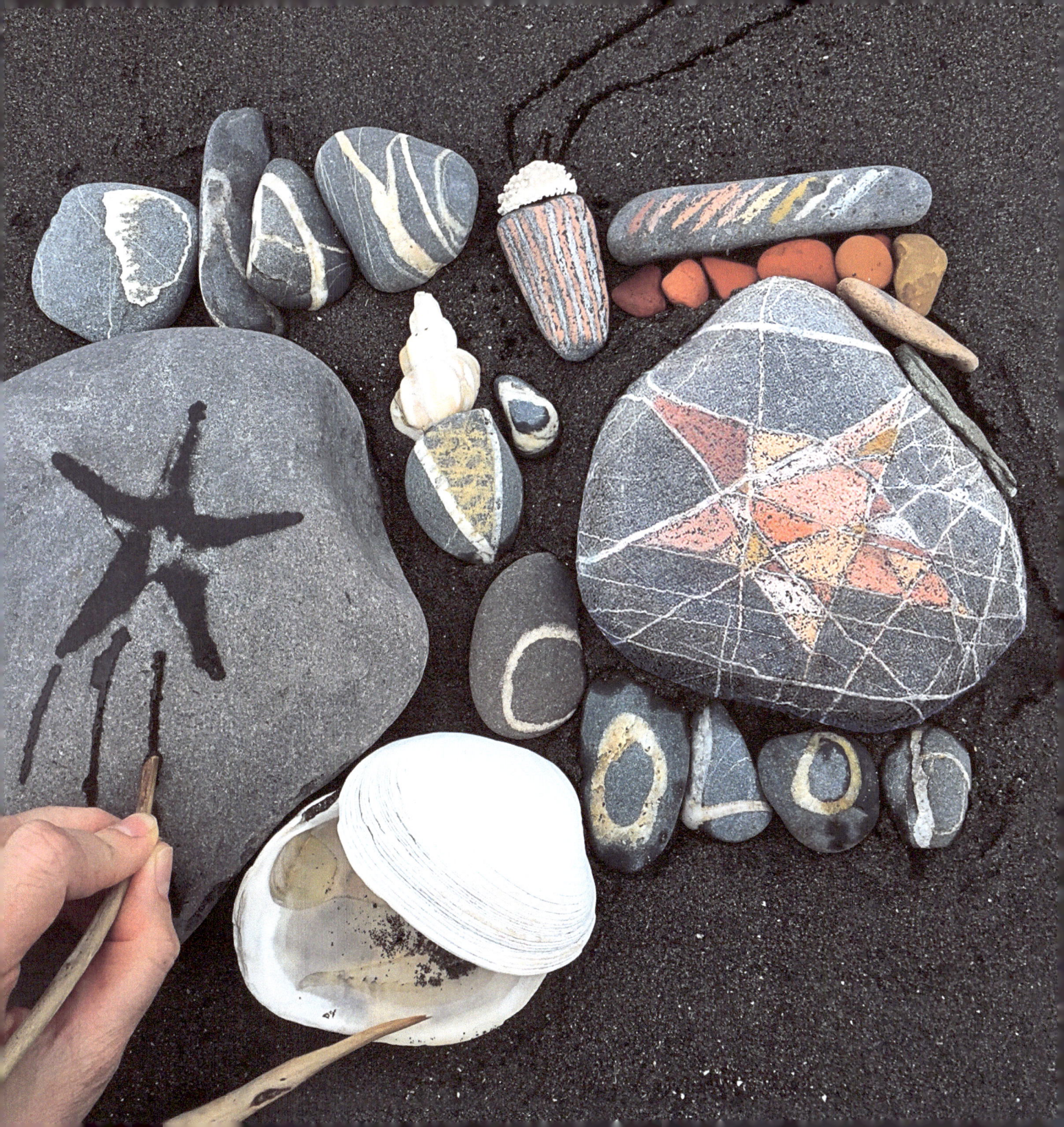

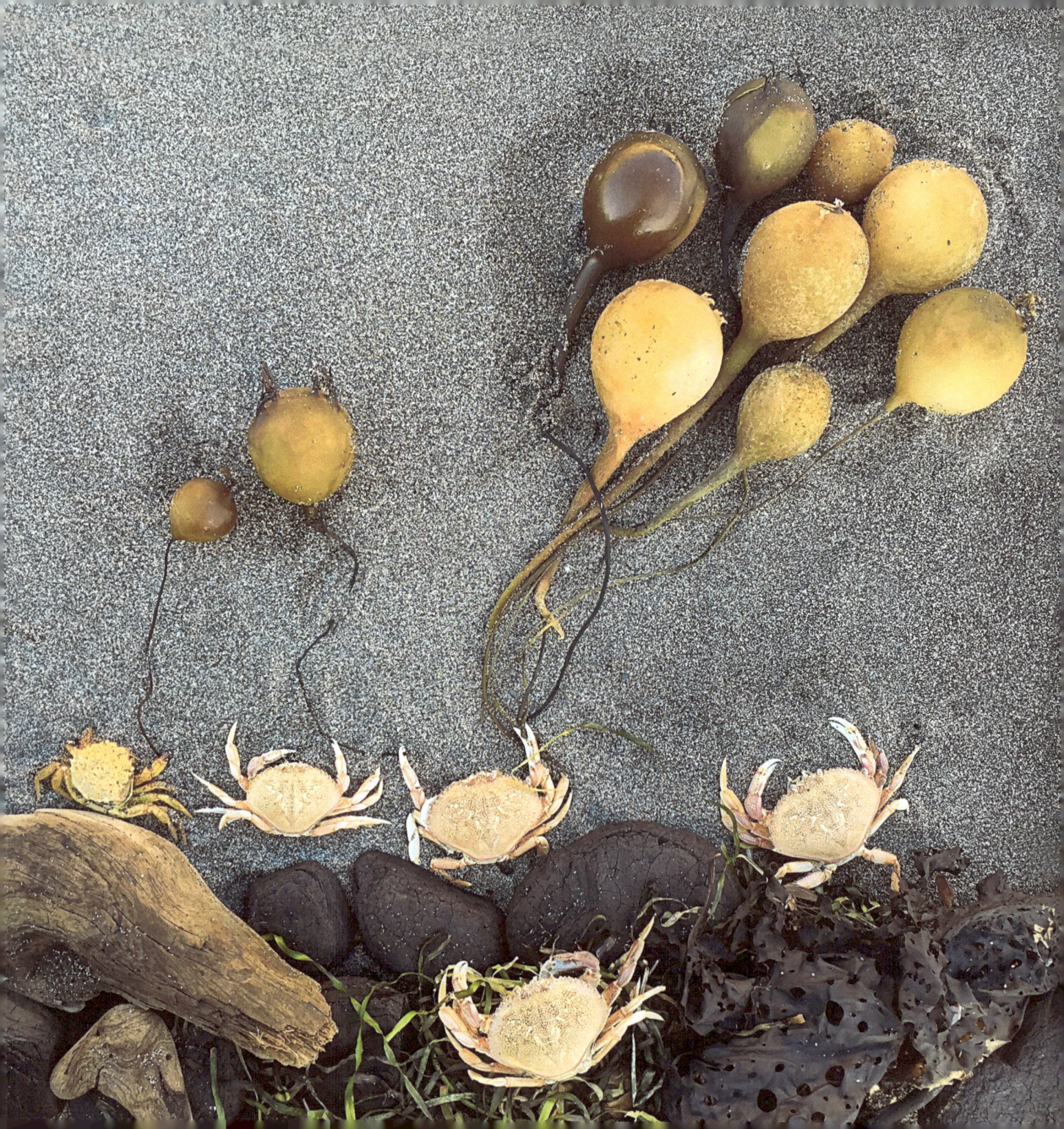

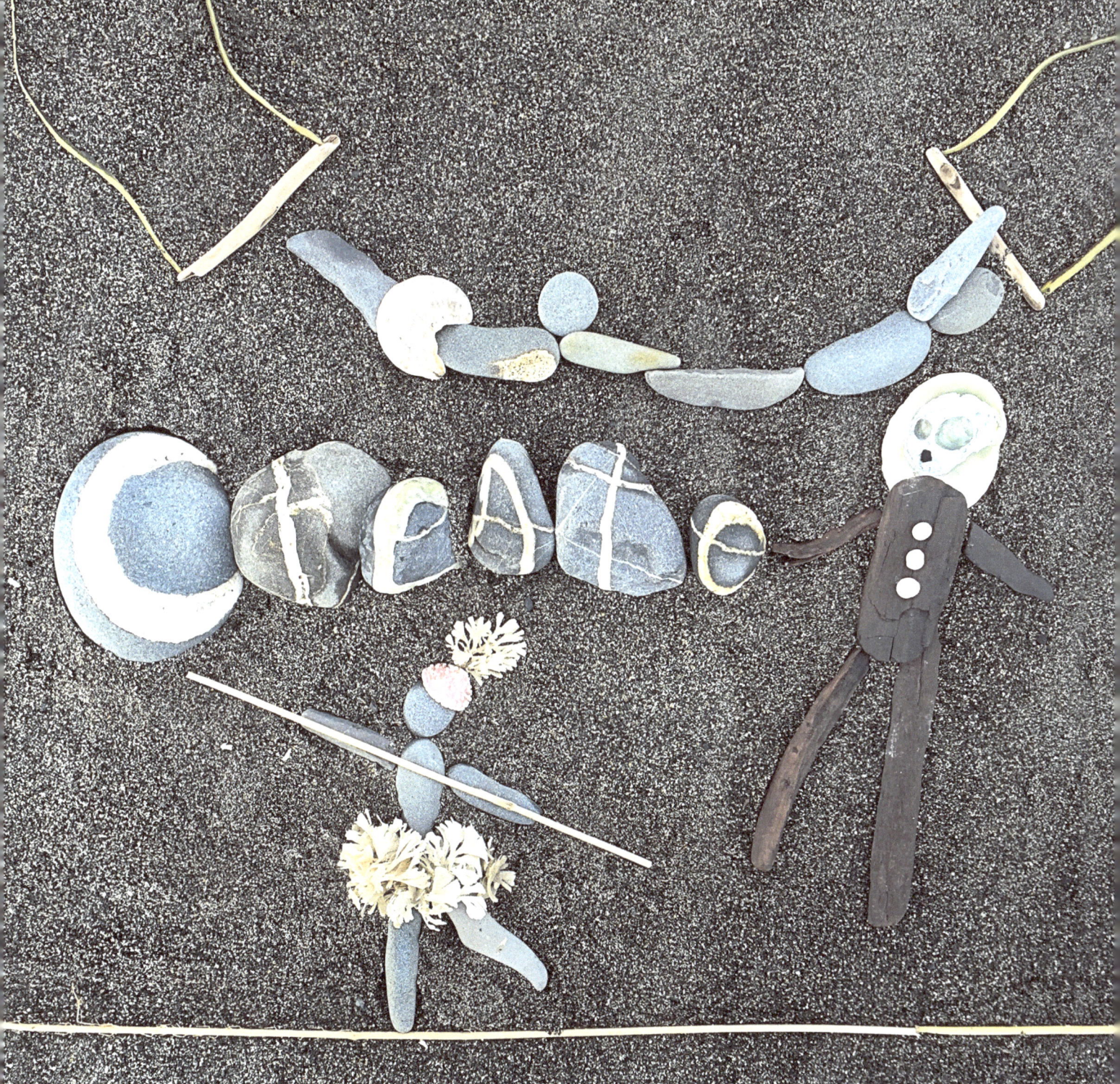

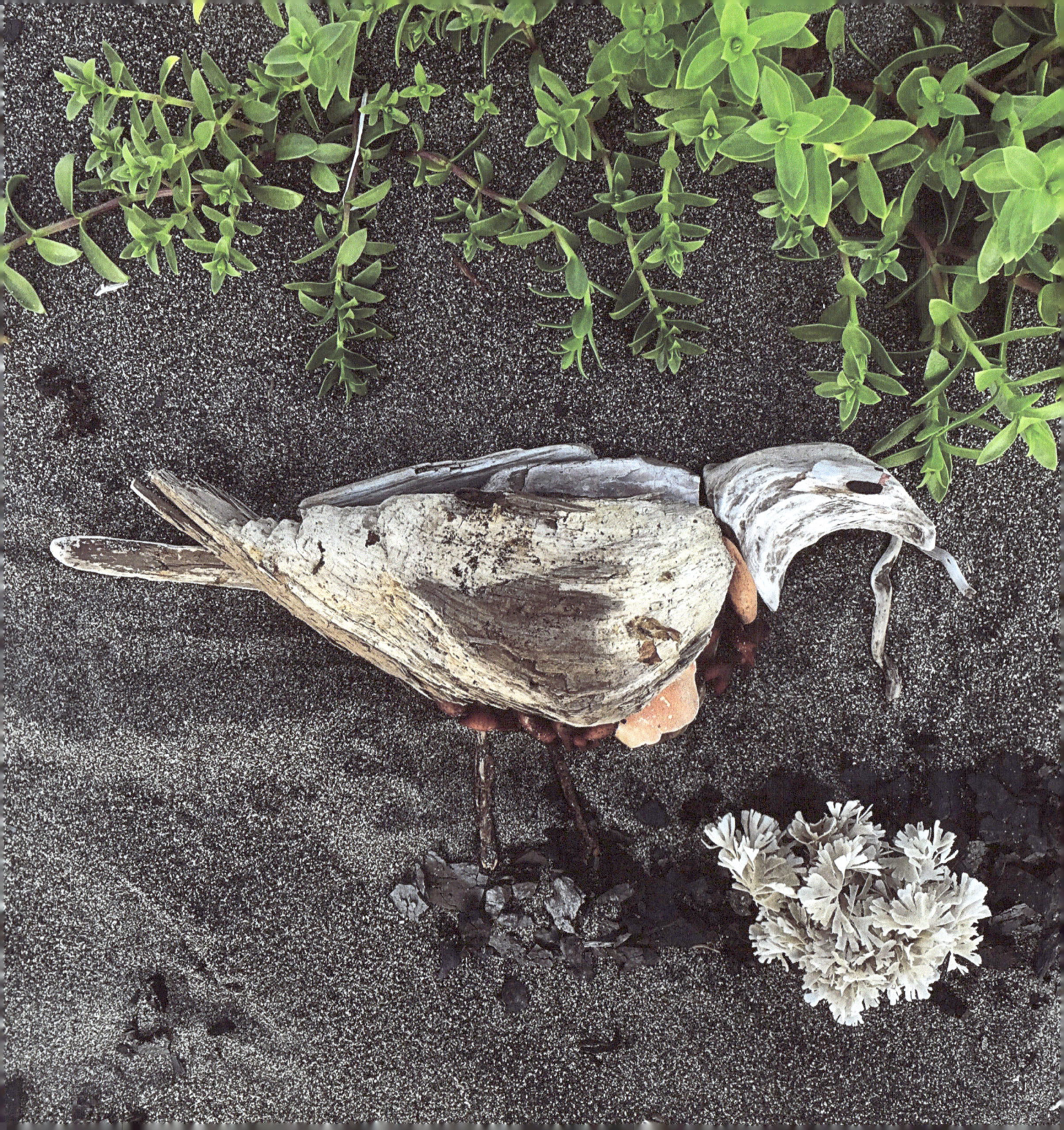

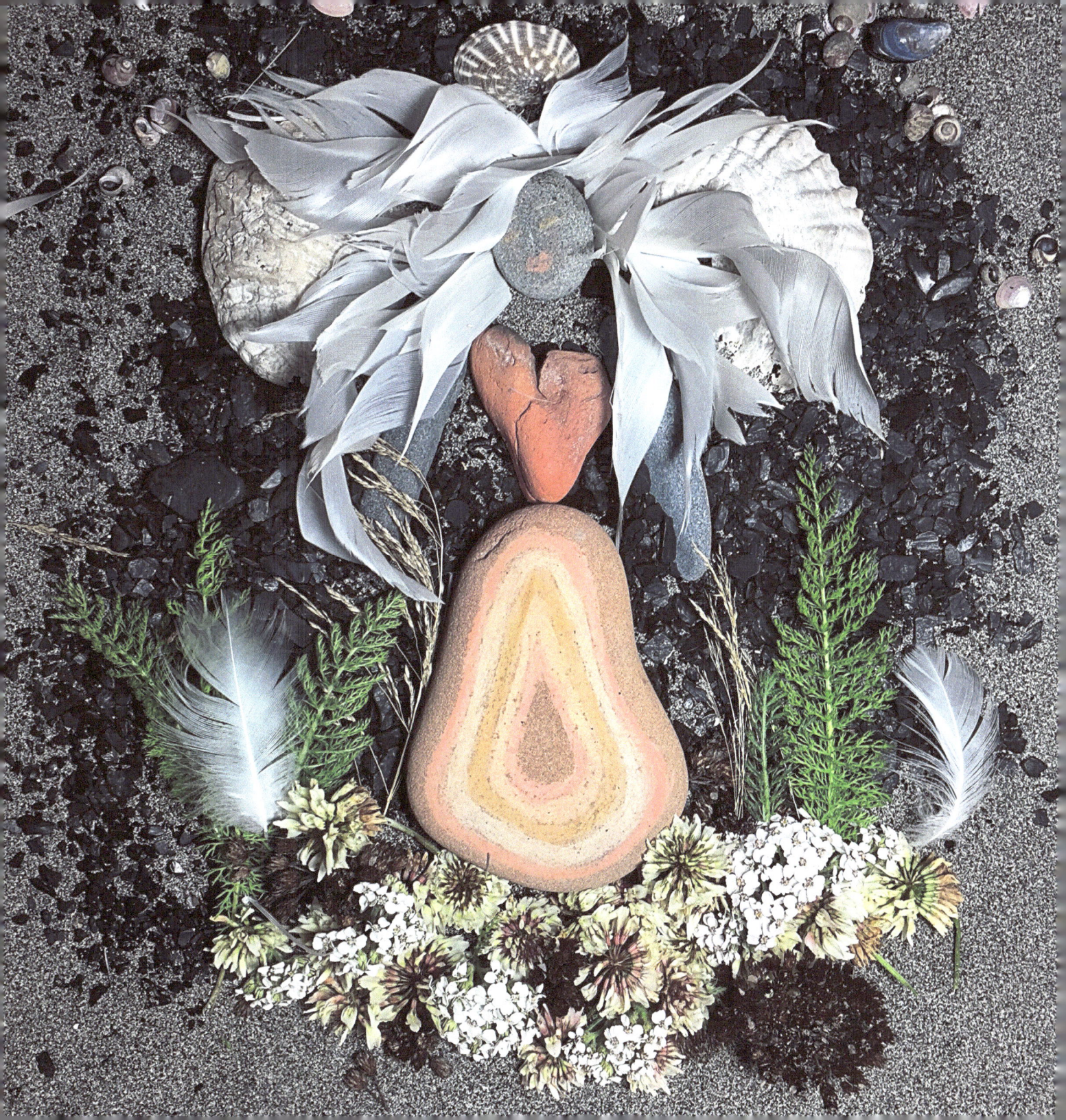

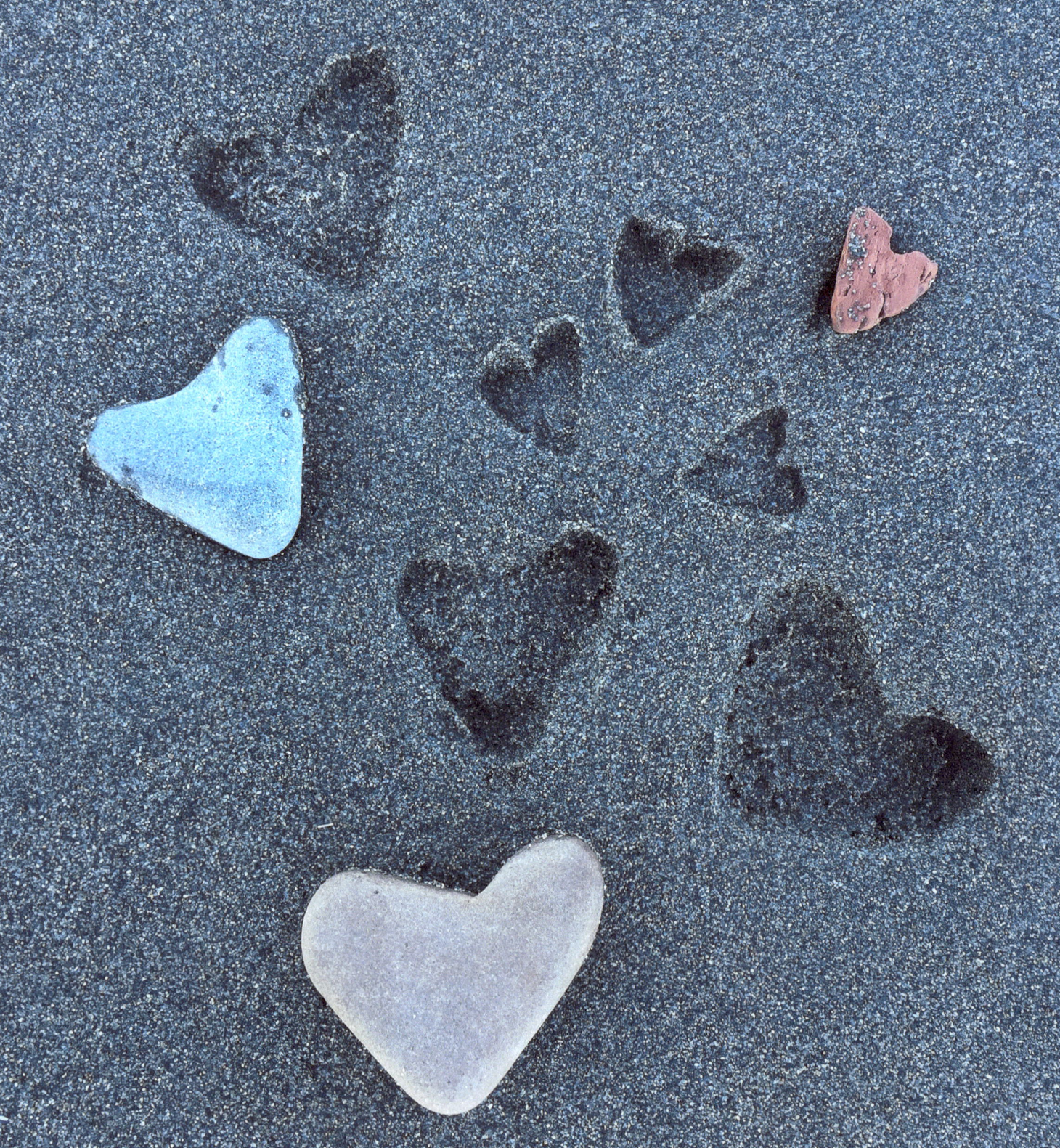

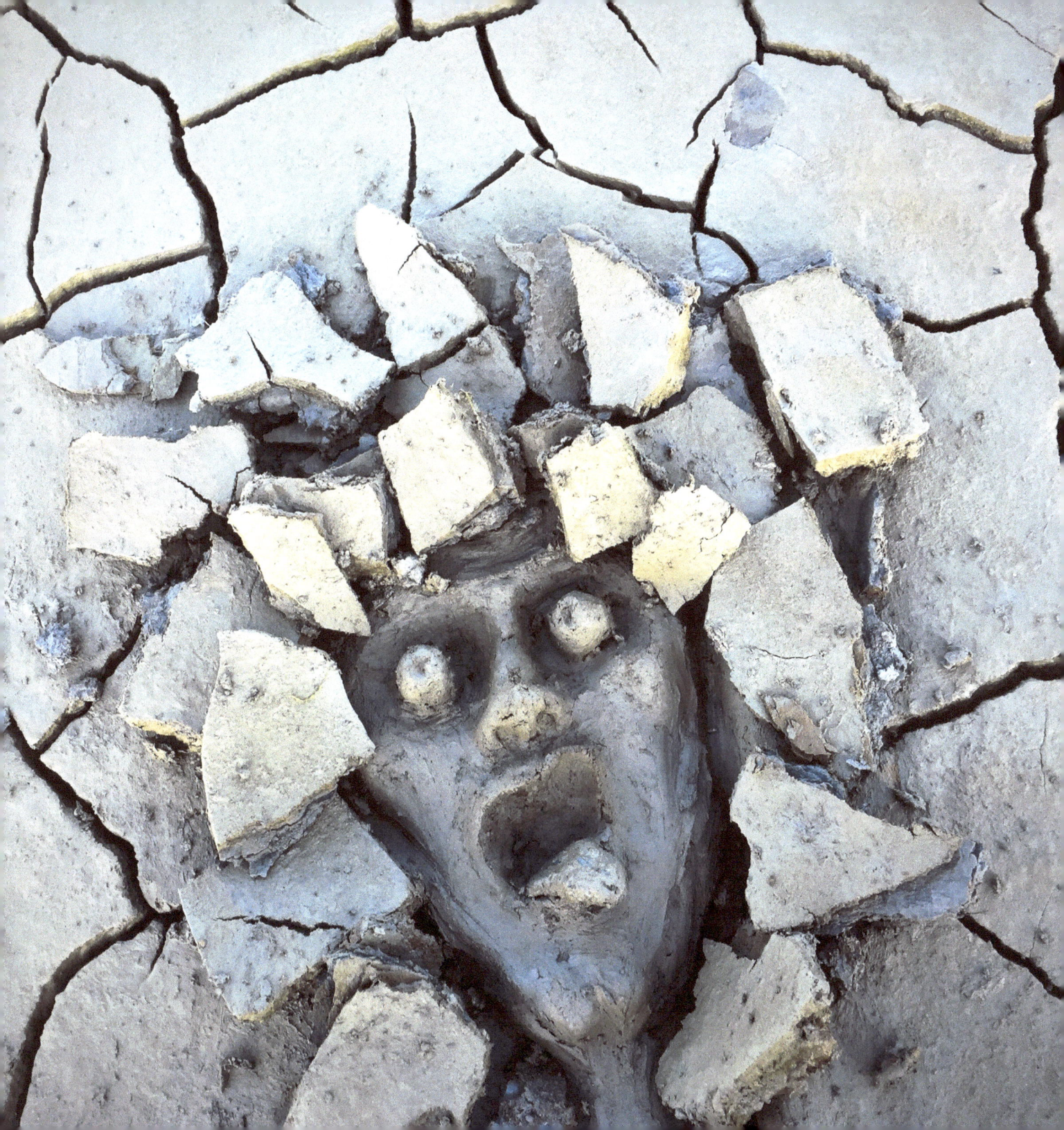

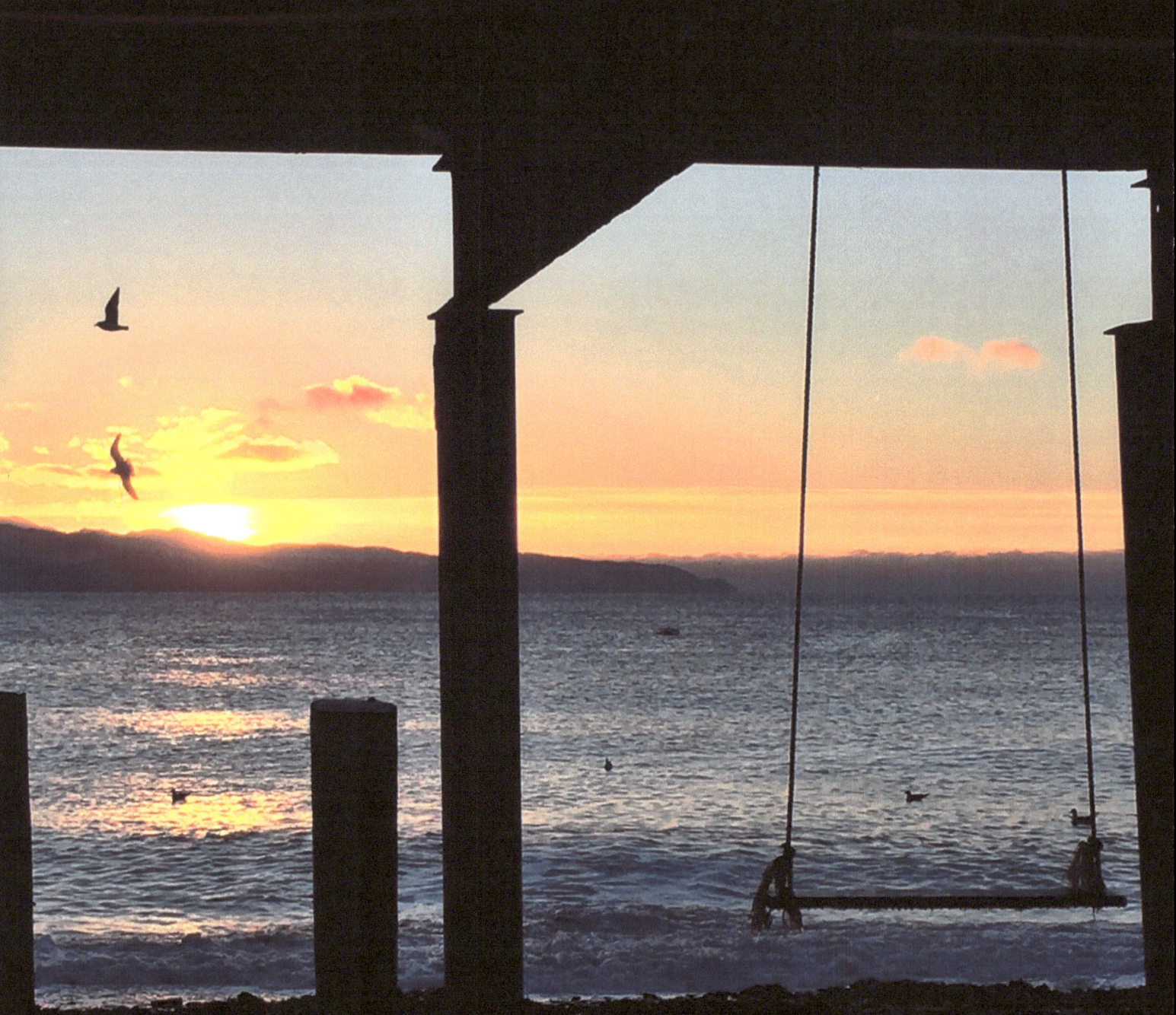

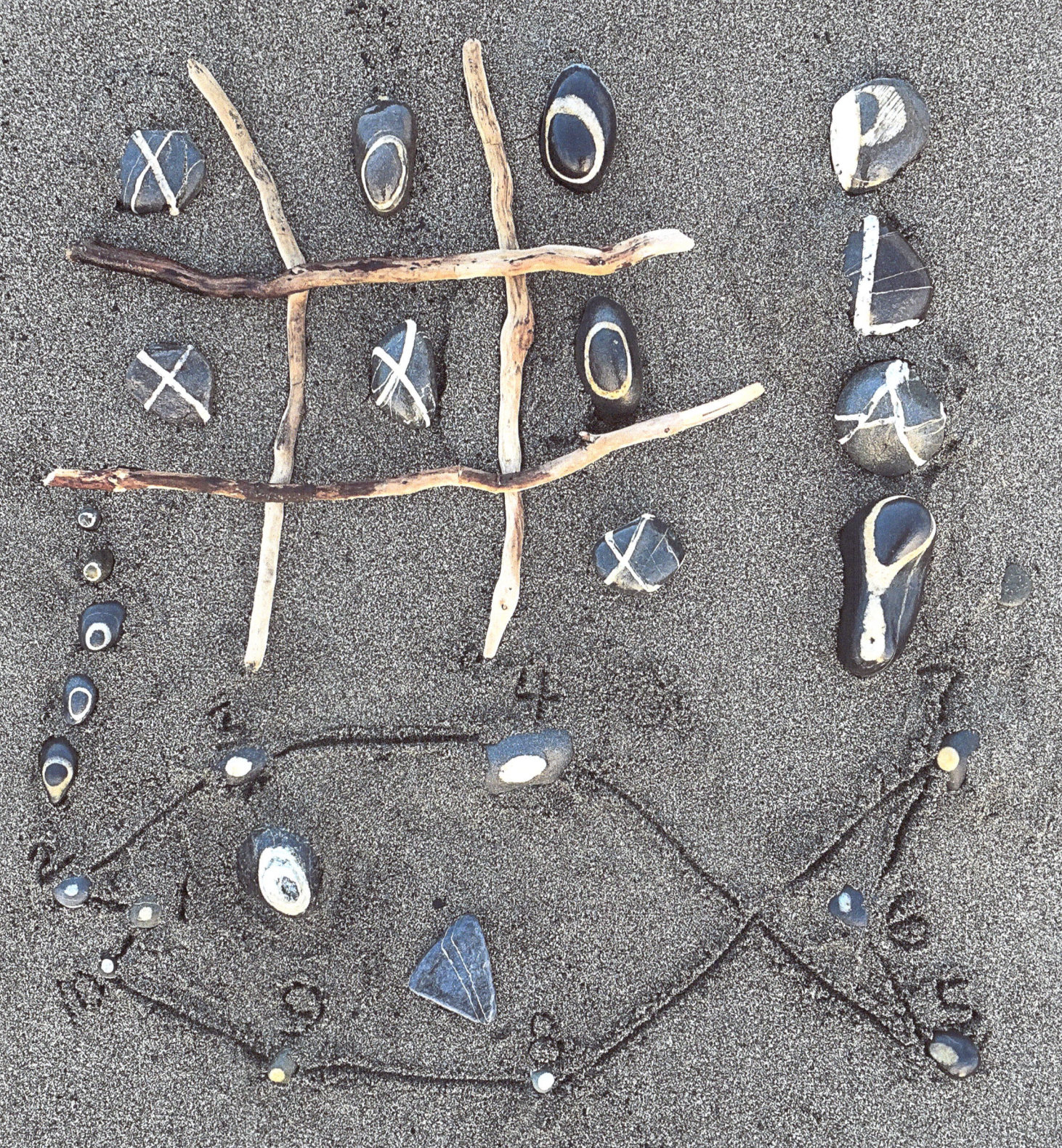

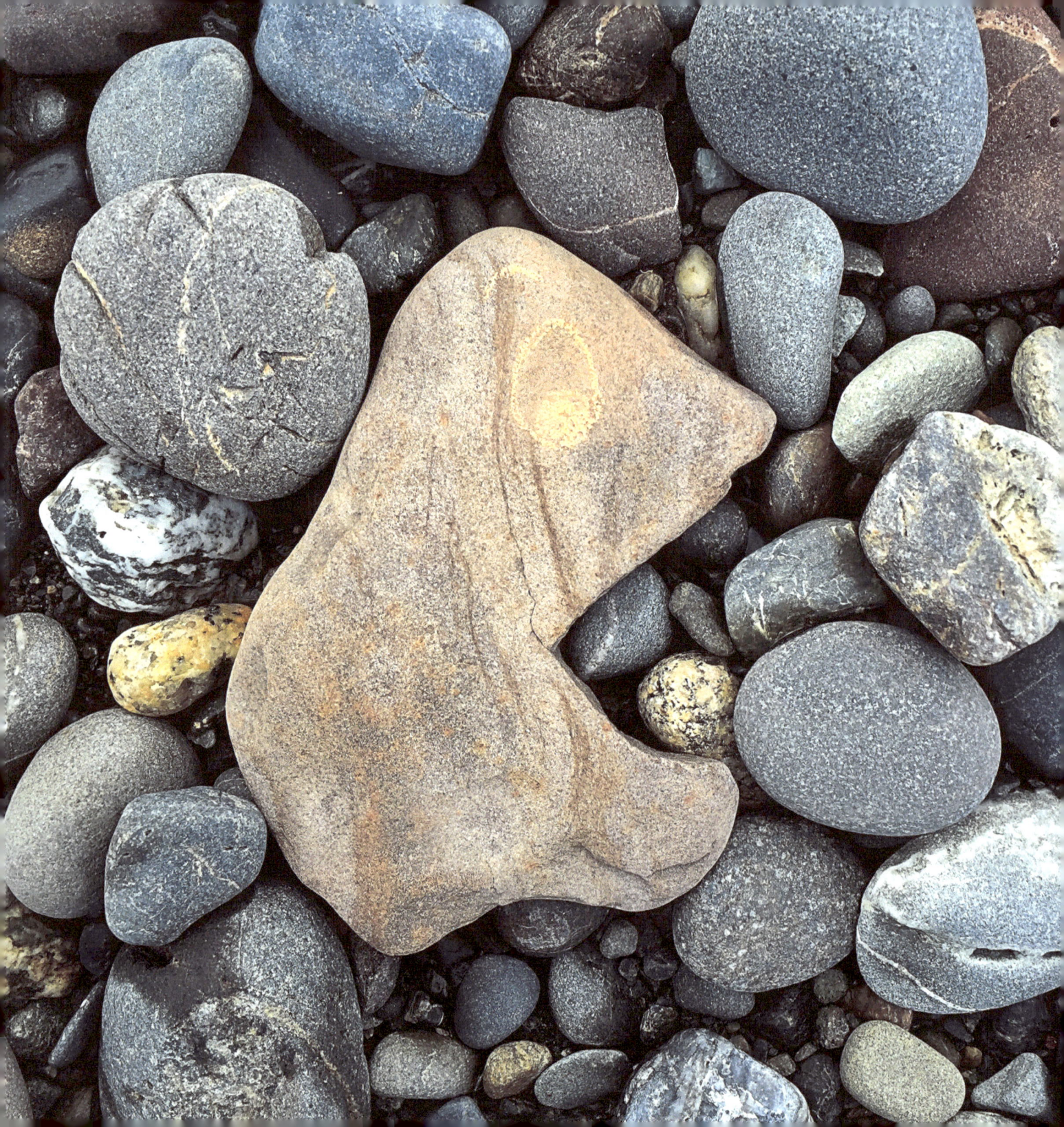

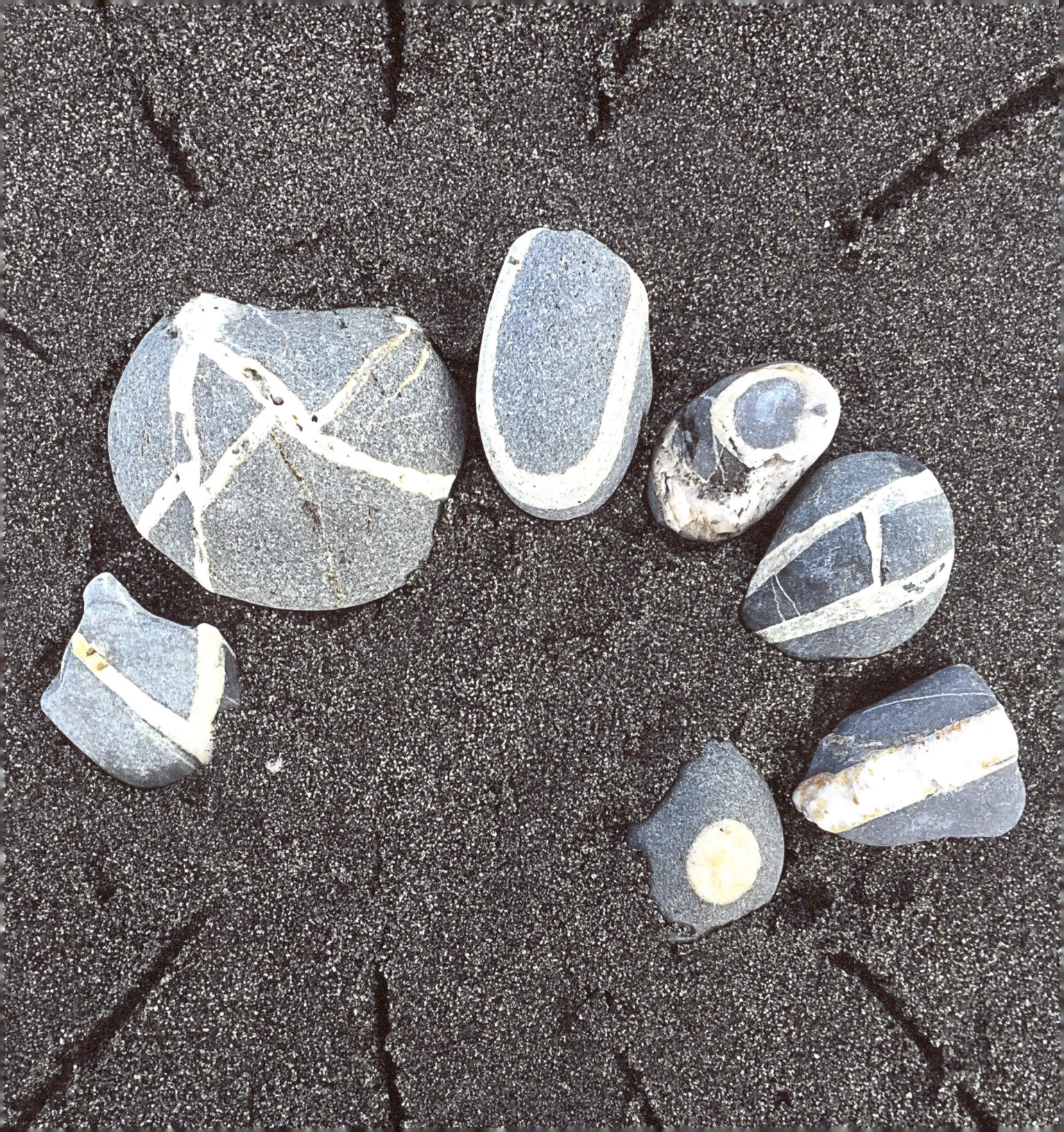

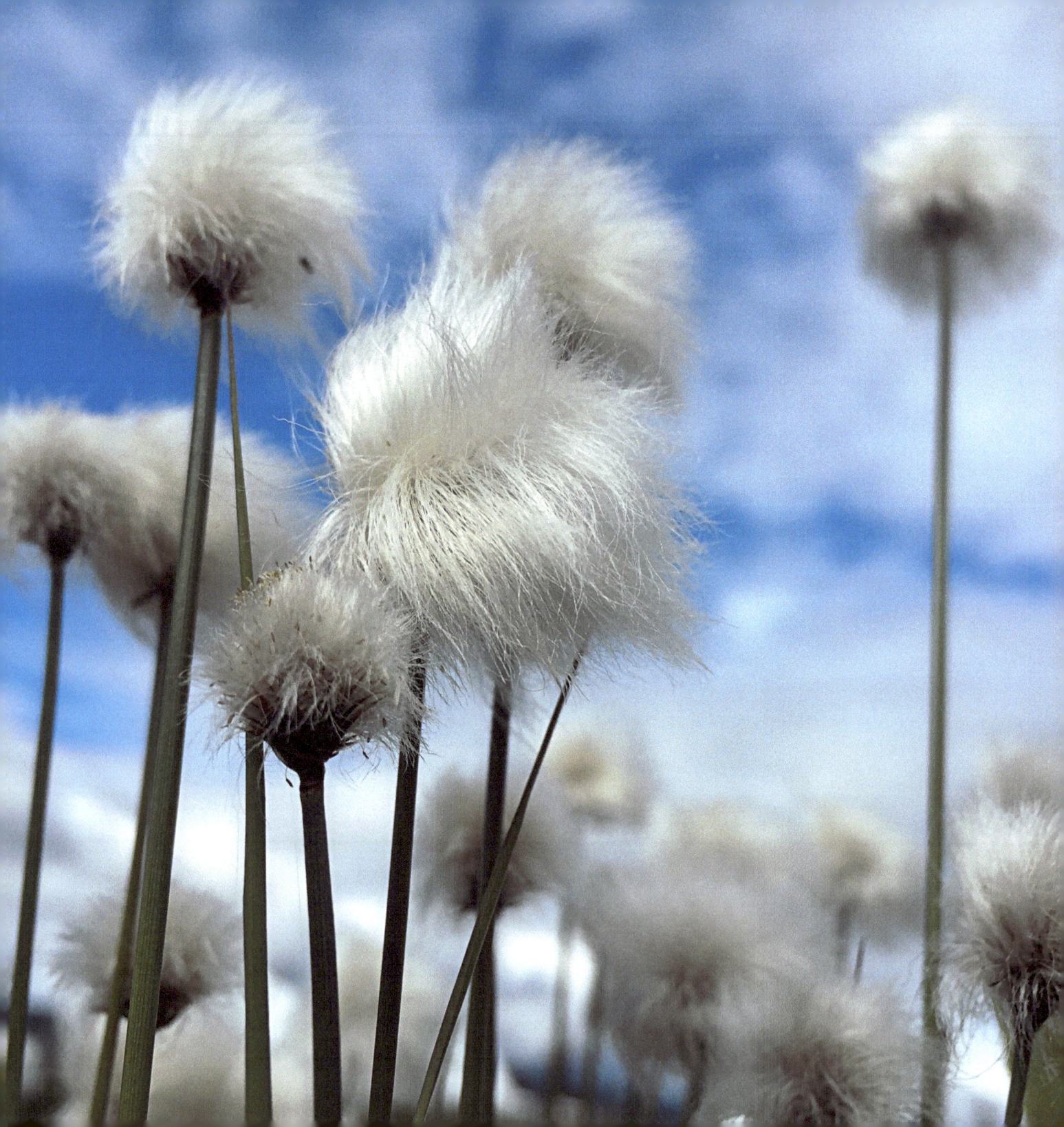

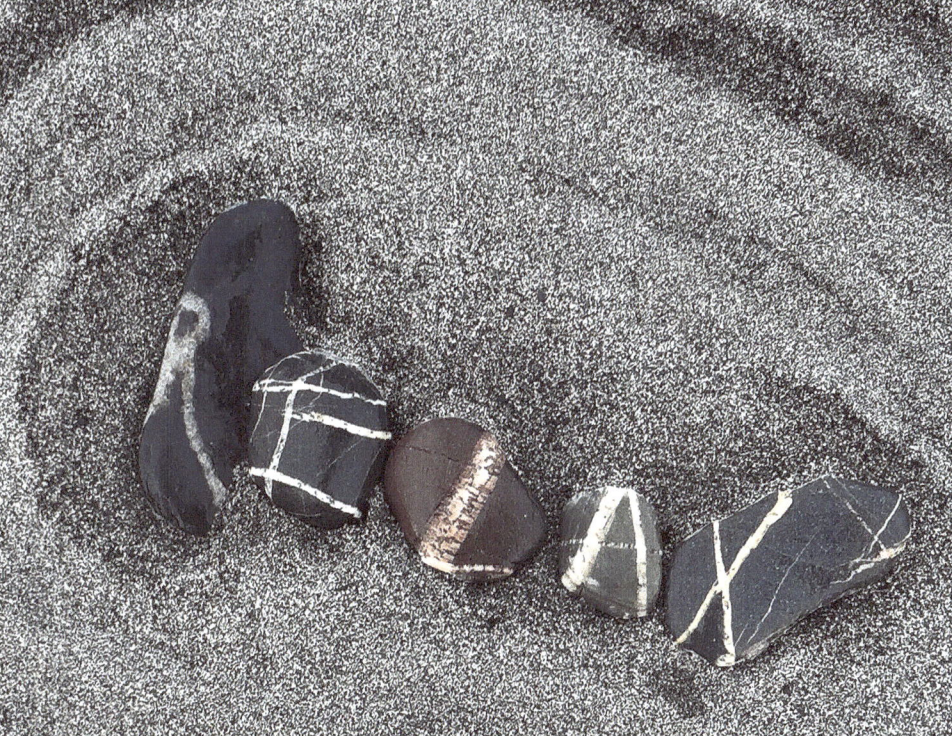

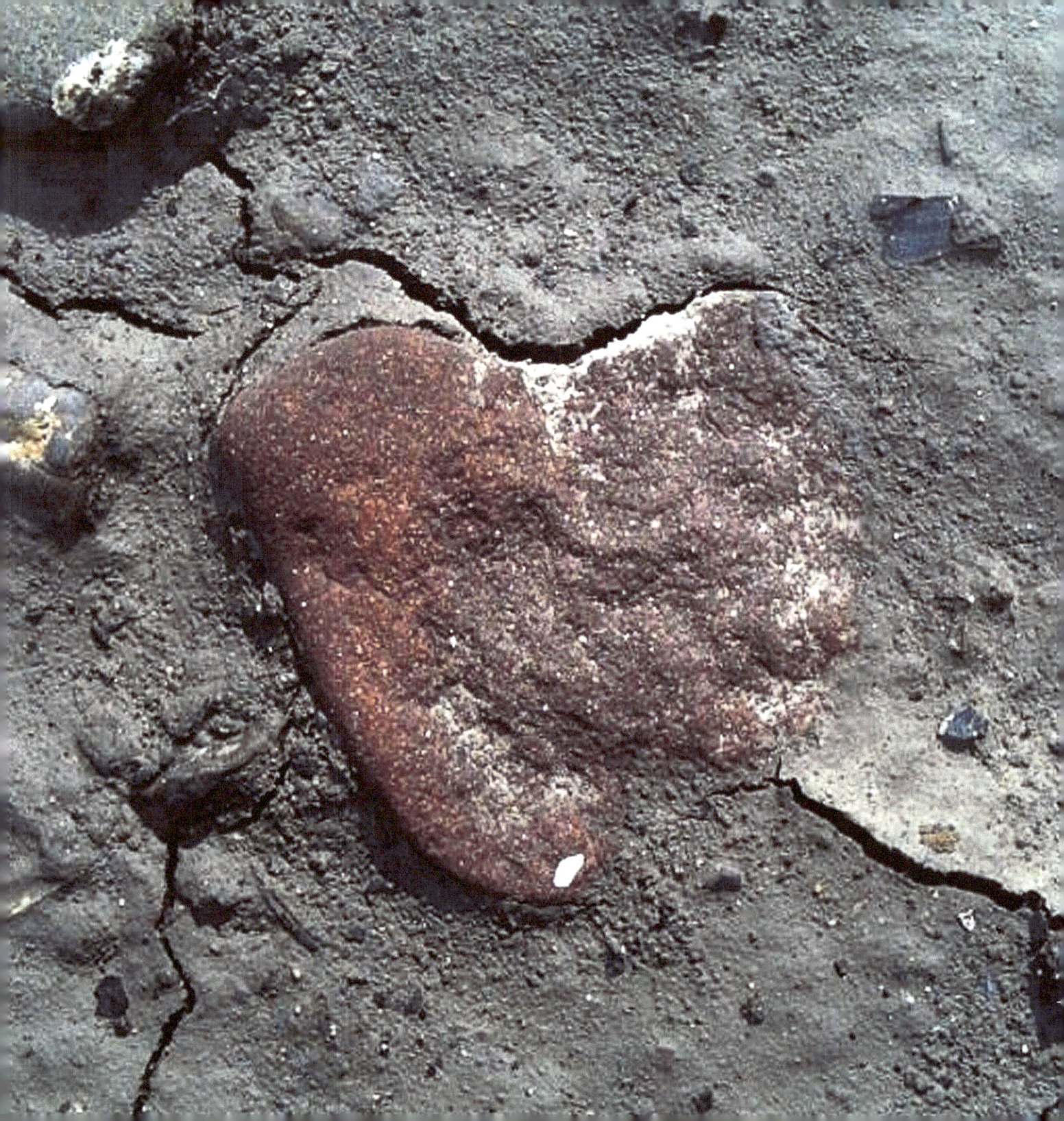

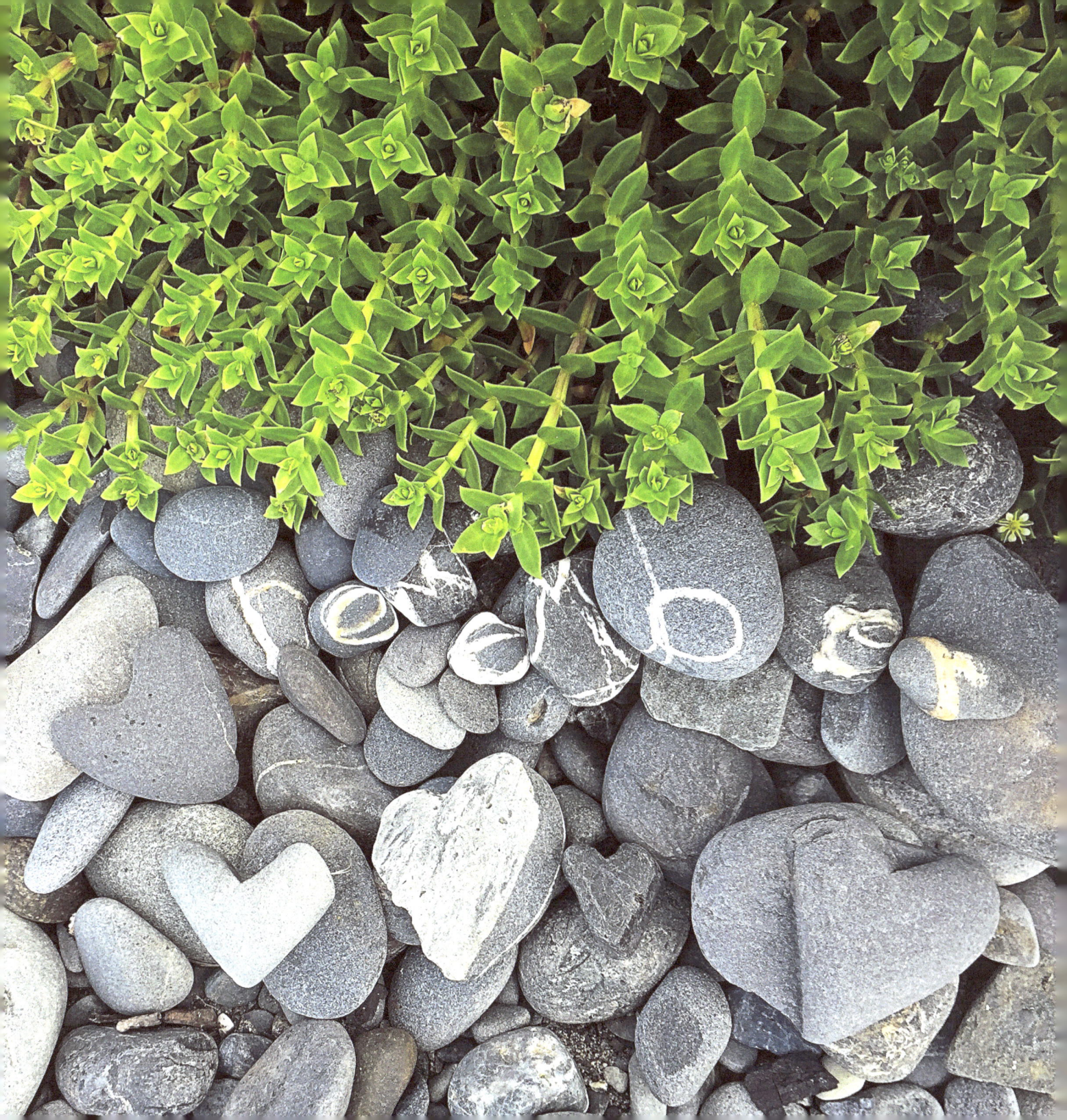

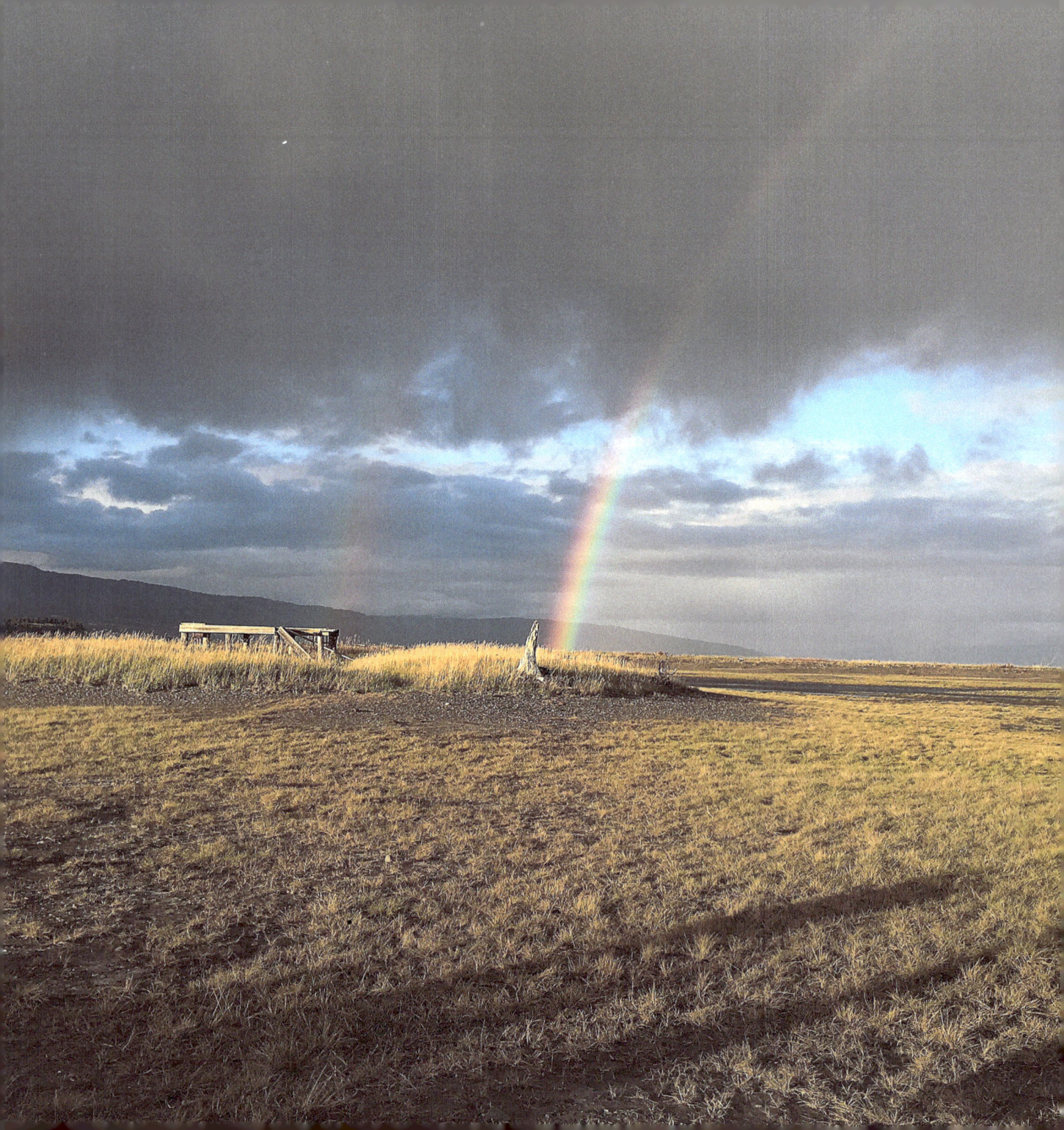

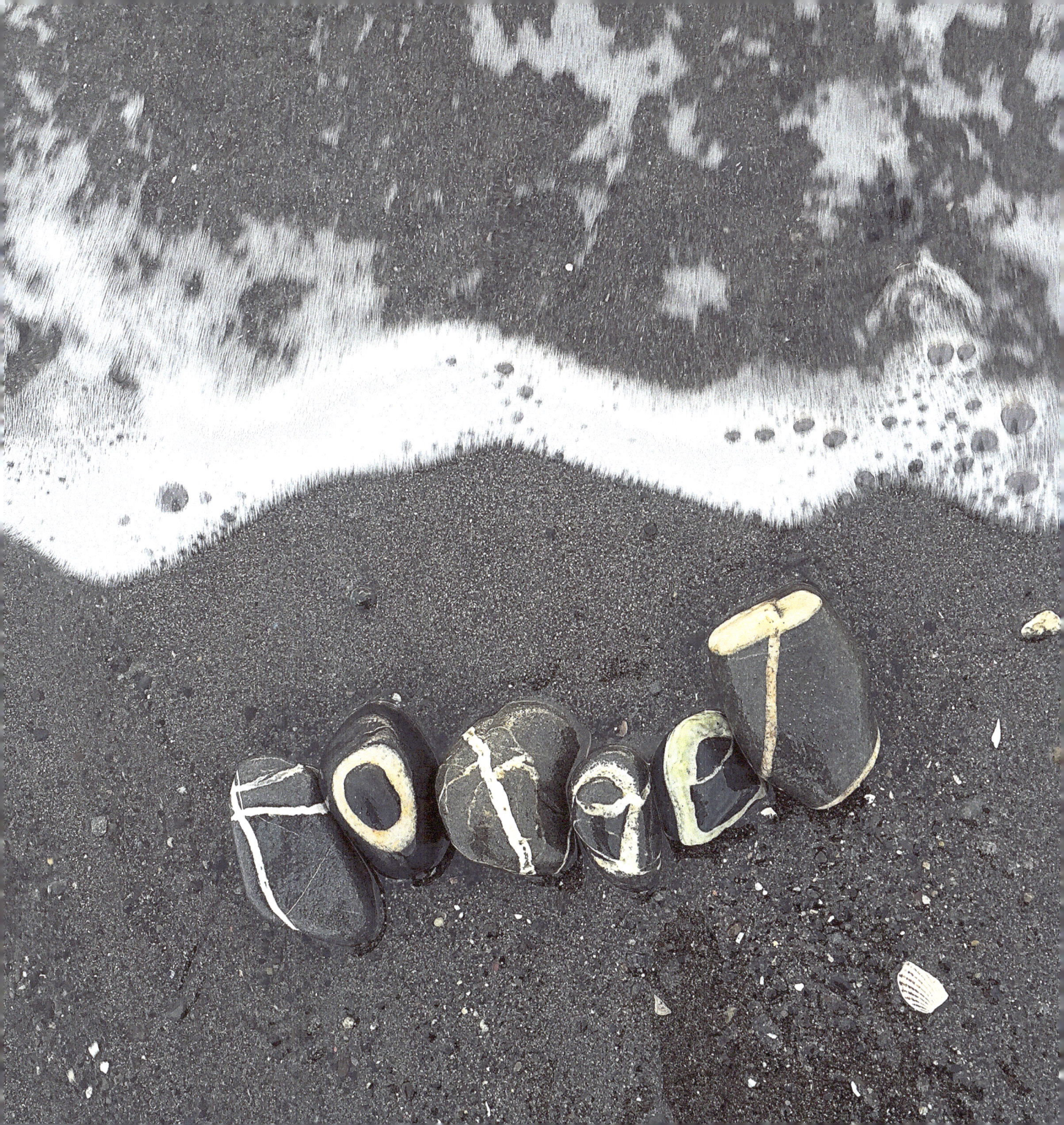

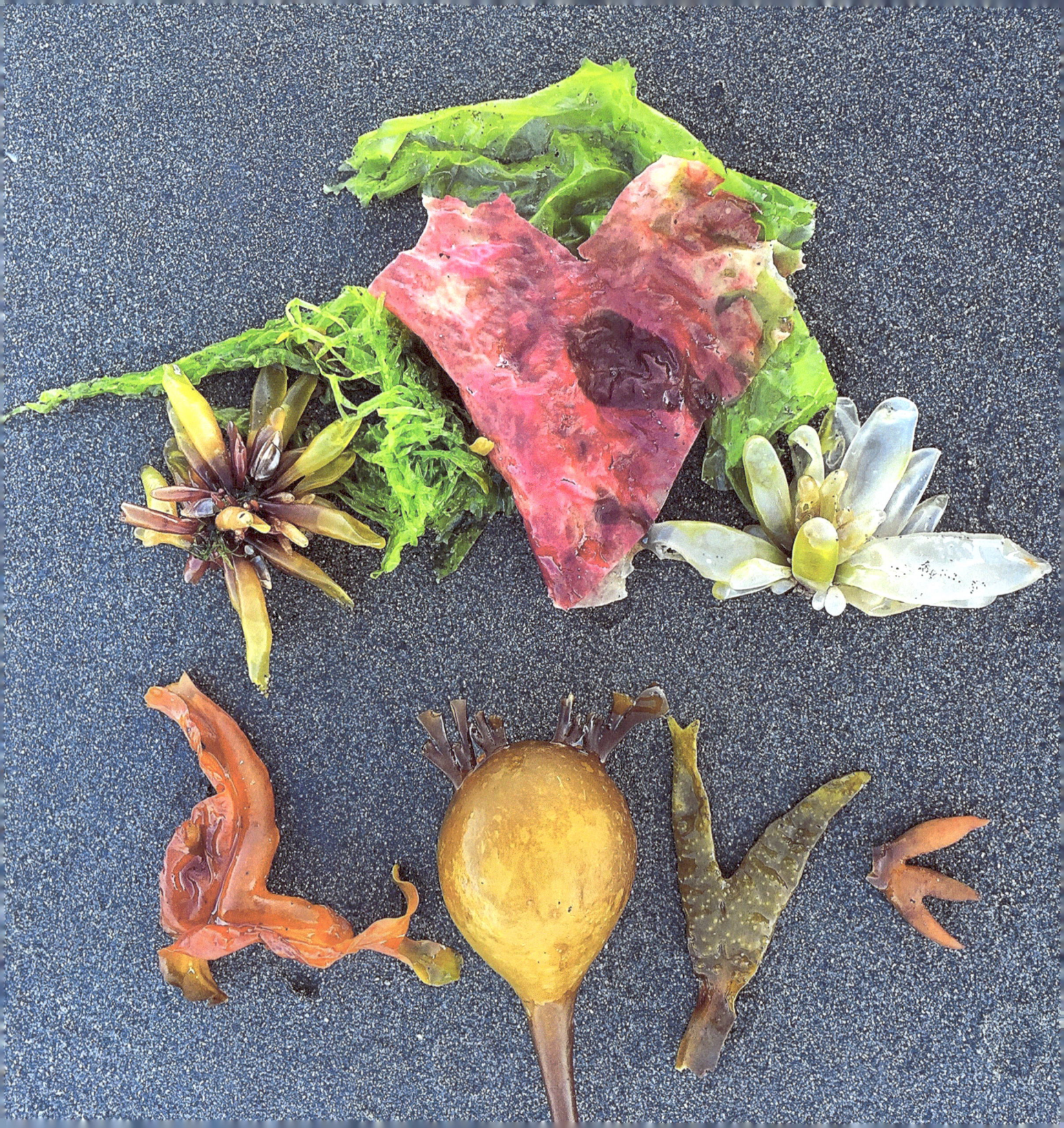

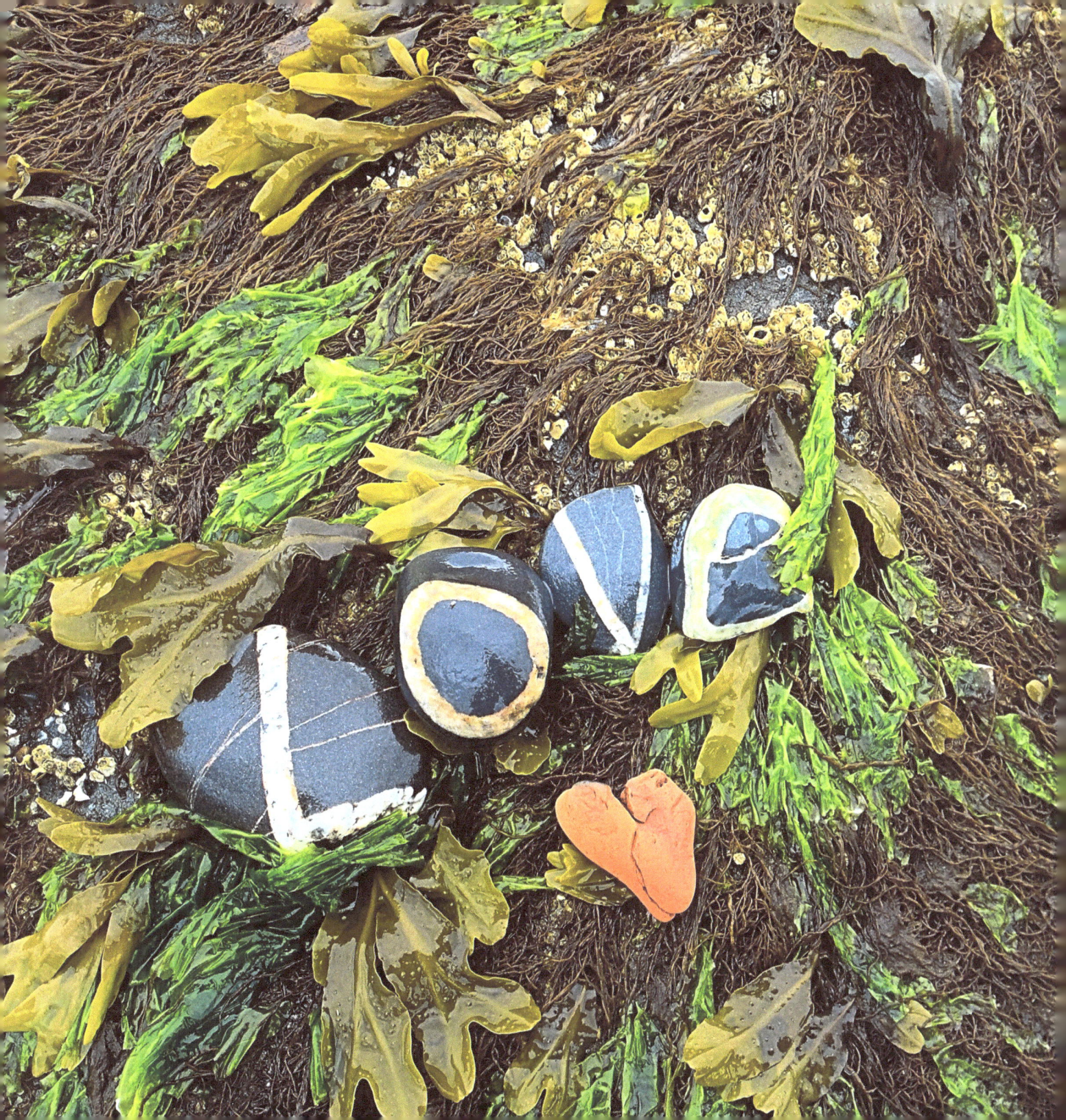

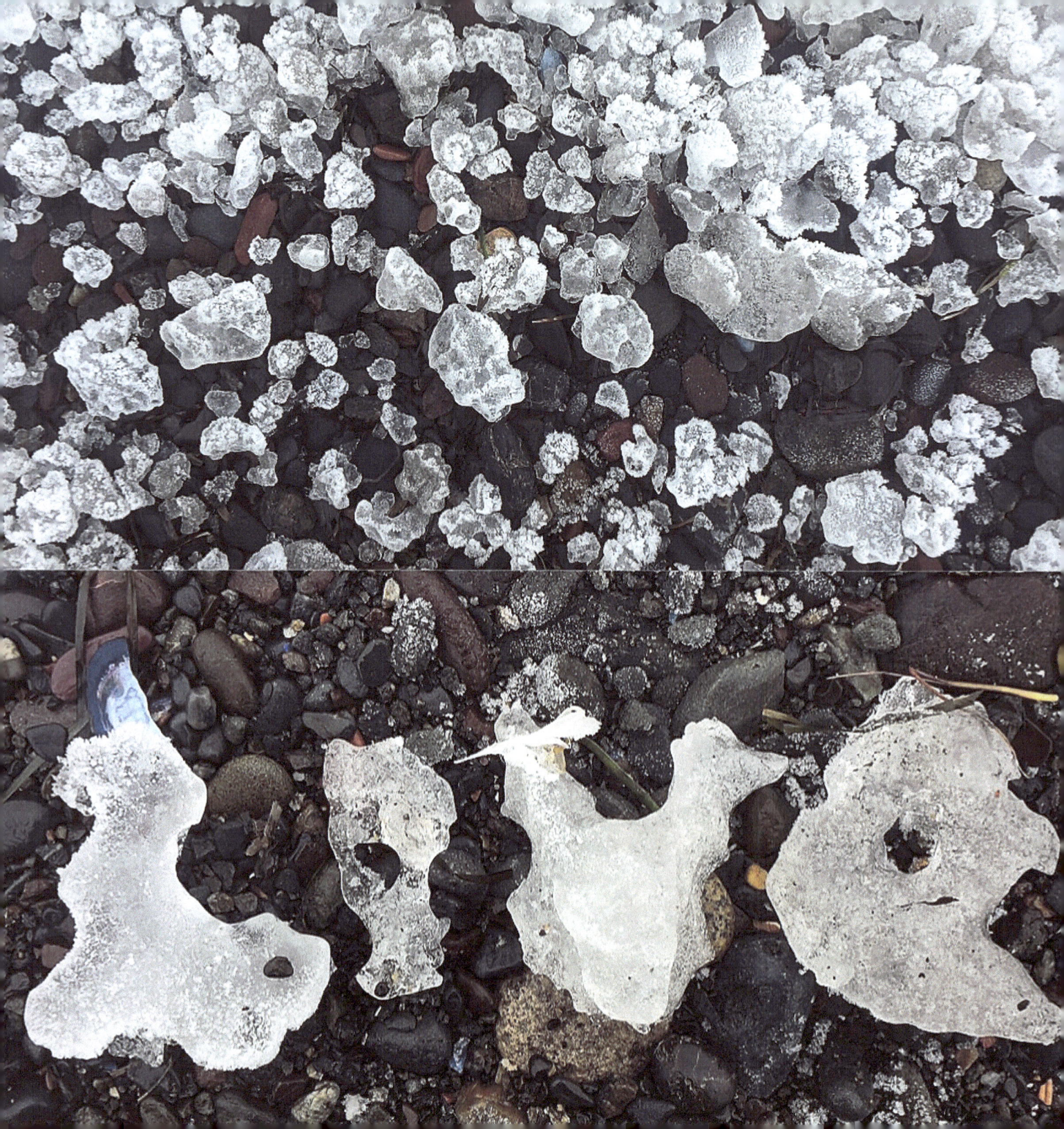

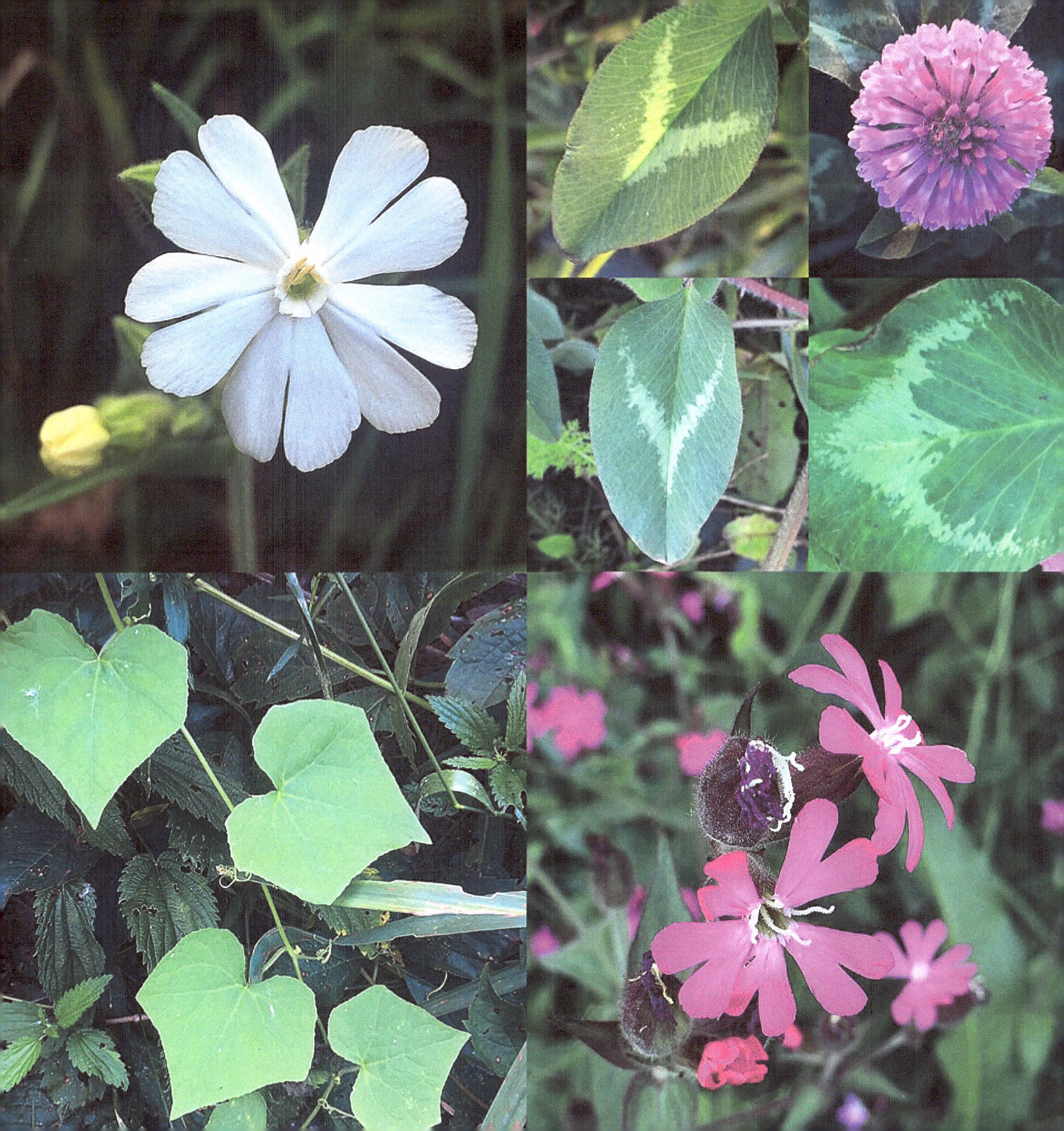

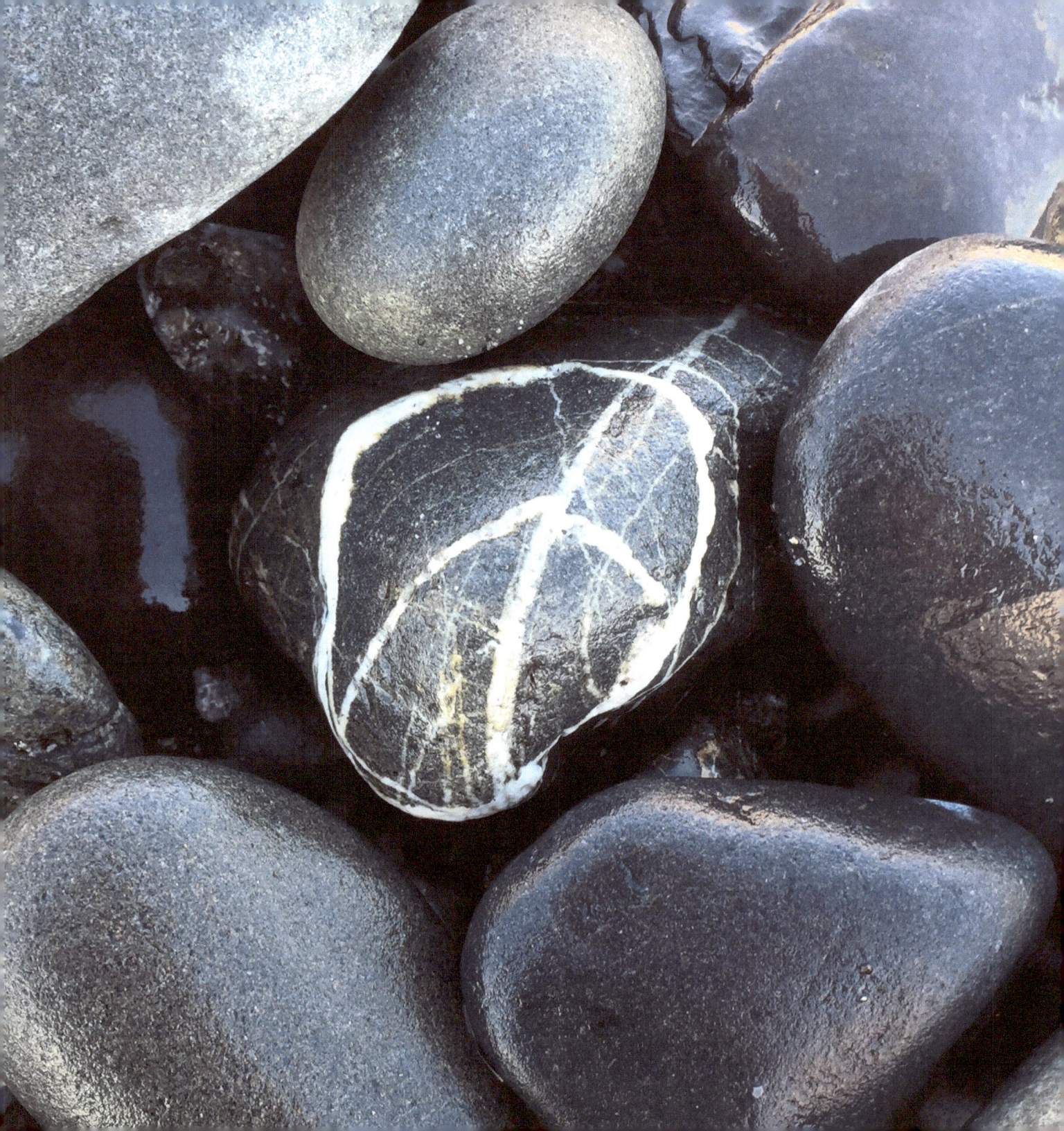

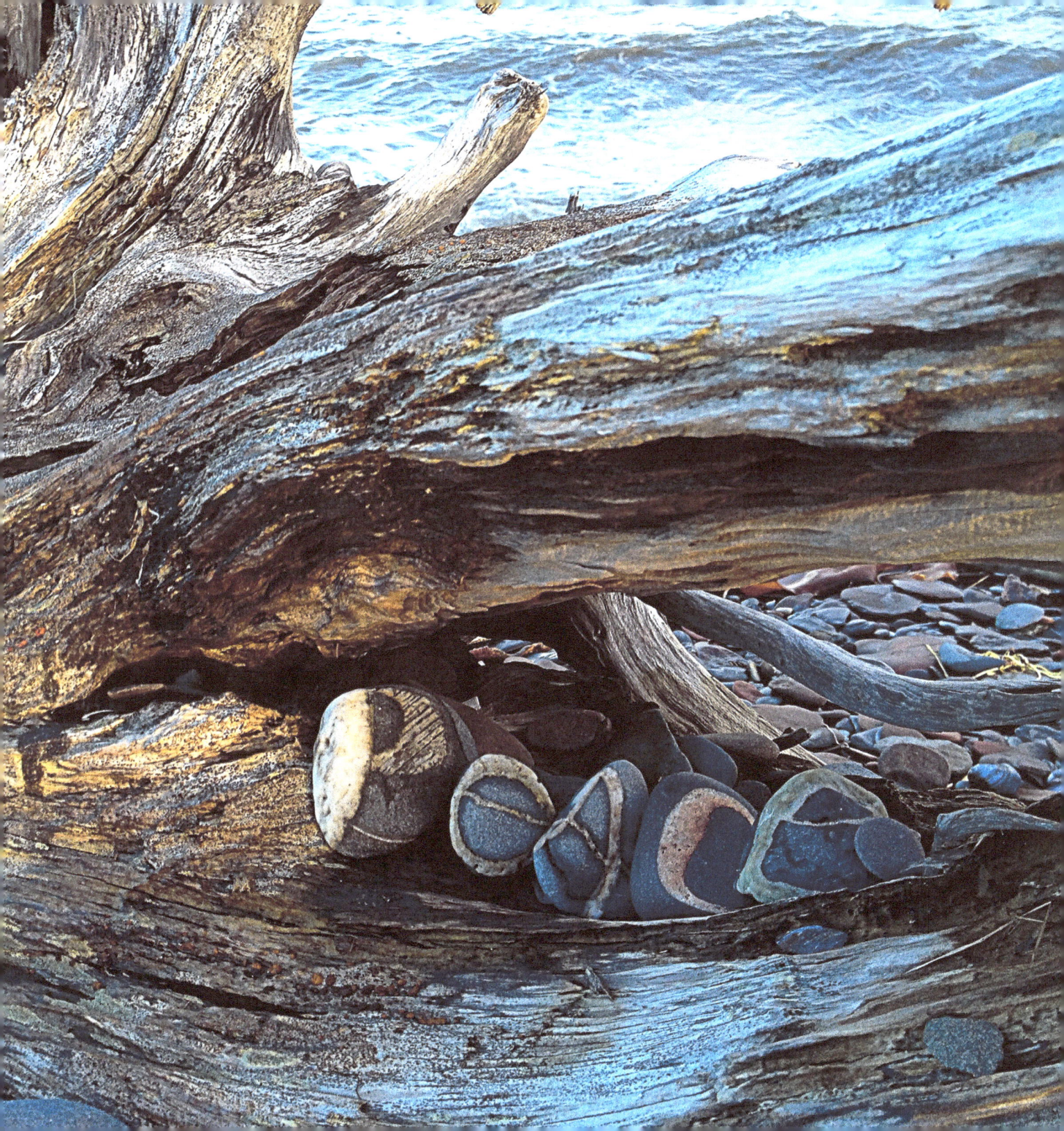

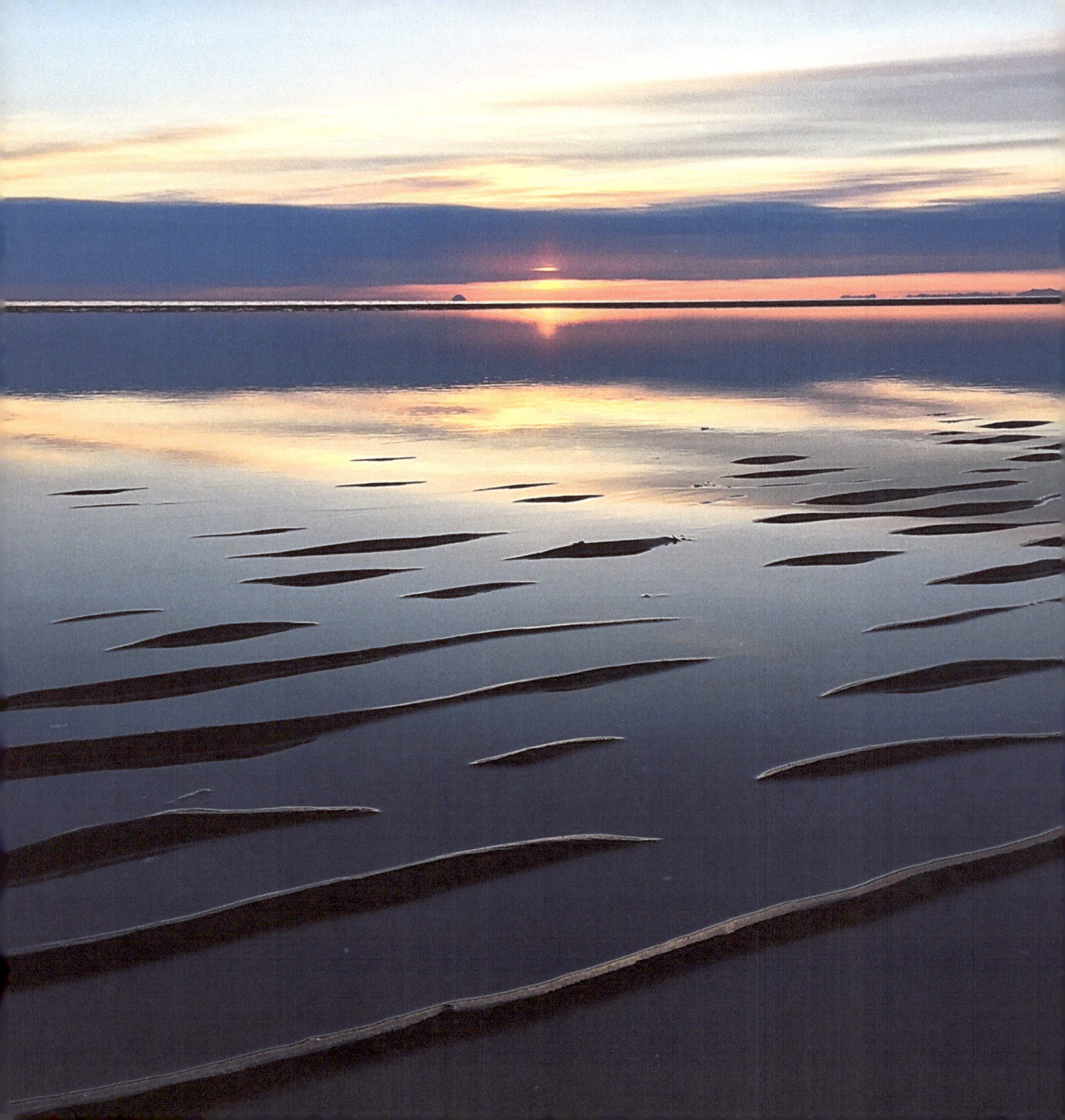

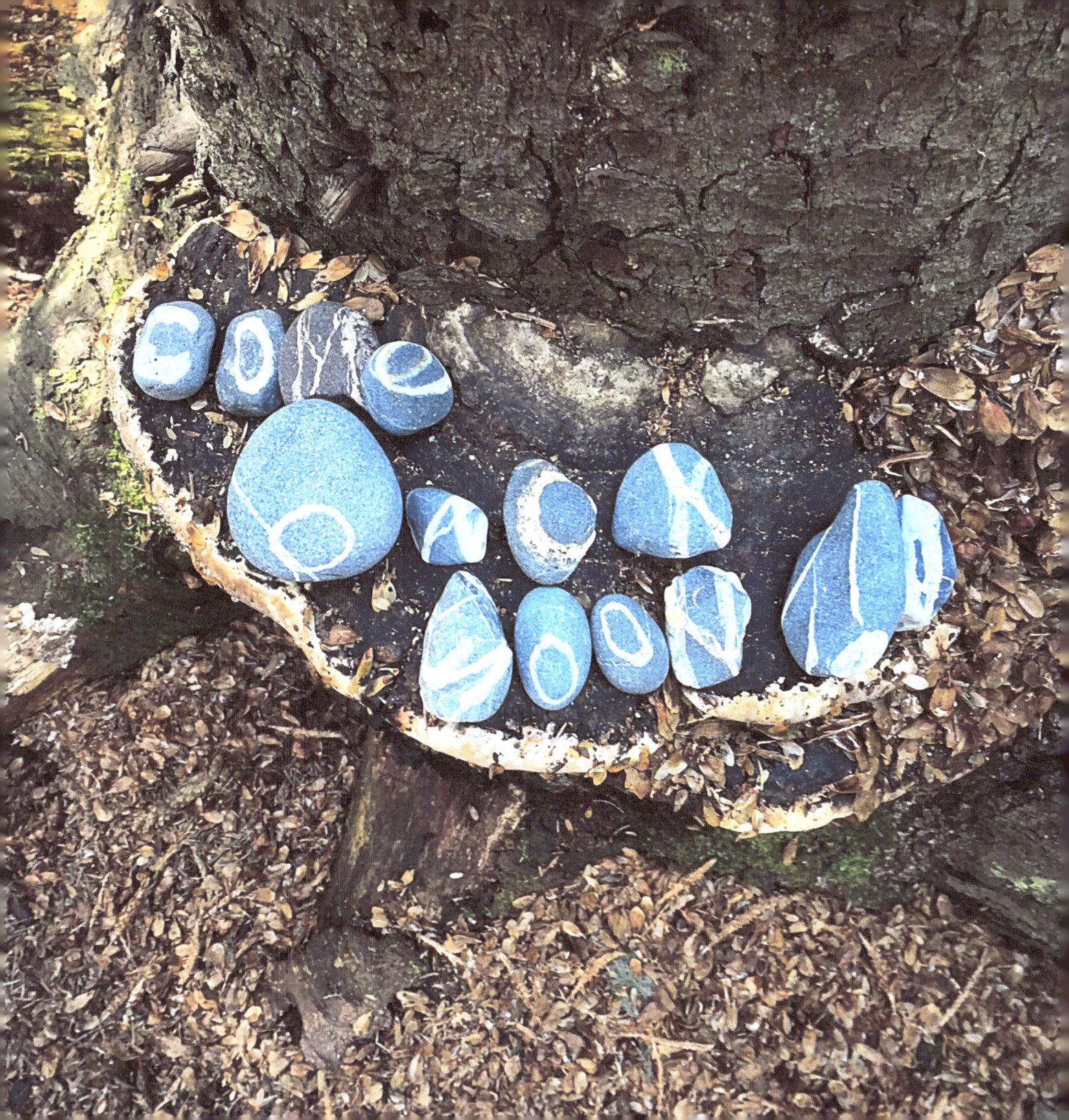

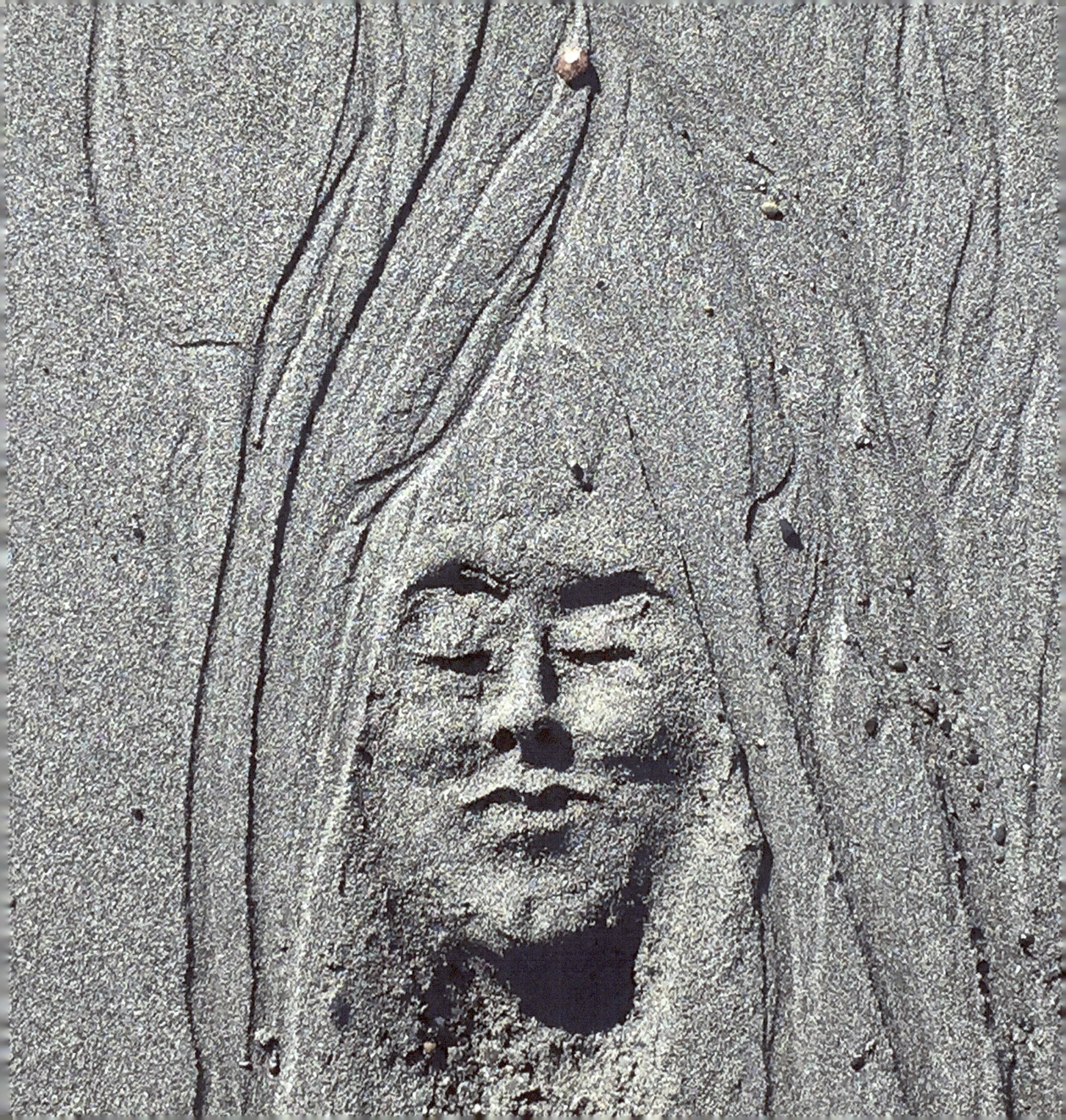

www.ingramcontent.com/pod-product-compliance
Lightning Source LLC
Chambersburg PA
CBHW051209220526

45473CB00003B/960